AN
ISLE OF WIGHT
RACONTEUR

DEREK SPRAKE

DEDICATED TO

The members of the numerous groups, societies, and organisations on the Isle of Wight to whom I have been privileged to give talks over the last 25 years and who have encouraged me to write this book, based on those talks.

By the same author:
PUT OUT THE FLAG
The Story of Isle of Wight Carriers 1869-1960

MEN OF CHALE
How village people developed their village in the 19th & 20th centries including two World Wars, from letters, diaries, etc.

Copies of all these books can be obtained from the author, Derek Sprake at Springfield, Town Lane, Chale Green, Ventnor, Isle of Wight. (Tel. 01983 551234, e-mail: djssprake@aol.com)

AN ISLE OF WIGHT RACONTUER by Derek Sprake
Copyright © 2018 Derek Sprake
First Edition February 2018

Illustrations by James Fellows
Copyright © 2018 James Fellows
E-mail: fellowsjames@outlook.com

ISBN-13: 978-0-9552916-2-3

Published by Coco Design Co Publishing
4 Bucks Cottages, Kingston Road,
Shorwell, Isle of Wight. PO30 3LP
Designed and produced by Simone Dickens, Coco Design Co.
E-mail: simone.dickens@gmail.com

Printed by Short Run Press Limited
Bittern Road, Sowton Industrial Estate,
Exeter, EX2 7LW www.shortrunpress.co.uk

AN
ISLE OF WIGHT
RACONTEUR

DEREK SPRAKE

Foreword

This is the first time I've agreed to write a foreword, and while waiting for Derek to send me the manuscript I began to worry if I'd done the right thing. Supposing I didn't like it! I knew Derek was a very popular speaker, but transferring nearly a dozen talks to the printed page without losing its original impact isn't easy. I know. I've tried it myself!

I needn't have worried. I loved this book, and once I'd started I couldn't put it down, and read it in one evening. Derek is a natural storyteller, with a wonderful sense of humour. His book, based on talks that he's given over twenty five years, covers a wide variety of subjects, from "The Funny Side of Banking" to "Self-Sufficiency and Goat Keeping", and they all made me laugh. Anyone who's enjoyed his talks will enjoy his writing. I certainly did, and the delightful illustrations by James Fellows.

Raymond Allen
Television comedy scriptwriter and playwright.
Writer of BBC sitcom "Some Mothers Do 'Ave 'Em".

ACKNOWLEDGEMENTS

The author thanks the following in the production of this book:-

James Fellows for his wonderful illustrations
(wishing him every success with his studies and future career).

Raymond Allen for kindly writing the foreword.

Lynette Atkinson for proof reading the draft, and typing
the script for publication.

Simone Dickens for preparing and publishing the book.

Ellen Weeks, and the late Noel Turner (who suggested the title)
for their encouragement in getting it finished.

Paul Kingswell, for much help and support generally.

Brian Greening for invaluable information when preparing talks.

The Isle of Wight County Press archive records when
researching the talks, etc.

Introduction

The author, Derek Sprake, is a true Isle of Wight Calf (NOT Caulkhead), his family having lived on the Island at Chale for nearly 300 years. Originally Mackerel fishermen off Ladder Chine in Chale Bay, this led inevitably to a successful involvement in the smuggling trade. They established the Star Brewery in Chale in 1833 combining these trades successfully in the 19th century.

His grandfather and father became Carriers for two generations, but he had a career in branch banking, mainly on the Isle of Wight. His interests included breeding, showing and milking dairy goats; horticultural showing; and running several local charities for the physically disabled.

On taking early retirement in 1992, he wrote his first book, "Put Out The Flag", a story of Isle of Wight Carriers, and later "Men of Chale". He started to give talks to local social and community groups such as the Women's Institutes; Town Women's Guilds; Church Groups; retirement groups; historical groups, etc. where he was soon in great demand, talking on a variety of subjects, often giving two or three talks a week, and donating any fees he received to the charities he had been involved with over the years. The main theme was to make it humorous and interesting, and to try and get the audience to have a laugh. Comments such as "… it's nice to have a laugh for a change…" from the audience made the events enjoyable for him as well. He has gained a reputation as a raconteur on a variety of subjects with a local history theme. As he says "90% is fact; the rest I make up!"

He was asked by several people who had regularly booked him to give a group of which they were members a talk, if he had written a book on these various subjects. With the onset of the three score years and ten, it seemed a good time to do so before it was too late!

The aim of this book is to sample the various subjects which have proved popular over the years, but not to give a full account of the subject; that will be for a future talk! He hopes you enjoy the read, and maybe it will raise further questions which will add to the interest of others.

Extract from one of many letters received over the years:-

"*Dear Mr. Sprake,*

Well that sure was an interesting talk last night. I heard every word and I'm as deaf as a block, but did I sense a feeling you were conscious of a few straight biddies dotted around. I reckon had your listeners been all male you would have felt a bit freer, in fact although you cut short the story of the Carter and the Mare we at the back had a good laugh (poor mare!). I also understand you made our rich 'Widder' smile, never before been known, I expect her jaw still aches!

Yours sincerely, K."

CHAPTER 1
Put Out The Flag

I had a call one evening from a gentleman asking if I gave talks, and would I speak to the members of his Club. He added that he understood I gave talks on the Royal Navy!

I had to say that whilst I gave talks, it was not about the Navy! On enquiring further he said this because he understood I talked about 'Carriers' and he assumed this referred to Aircraft Carriers. I had to explain that my Carriers were the old Country Carriers who travelled between villages and market towns, collecting and delivering goods; doing people's shopping; and taking passengers along routes not covered by Stage Coaches. "That'll do" he said.

With that possibility of confusion, and the clear indication that many of my audience had no idea of what I was talking about, an explanation was usually necessary. Older people clearly remembered the Carriers calling, but younger ones had no idea. I usually start by saying that I was not talking about the Navy (Aircraft Carriers); indeed I was not talking about Supermarket bags; or people who might transmit diseases; my Carriers were the Country Carriers who for centuries worked in the country districts here on the Isle of Wight, but also all over the Country; indeed, at times all over the world.

Both my father and grandfather were Carriers from 1895 to 1964 and this was a trade close to my heart all my life.

The origins of the trade were probably with Peddlers who passed from village to village selling or 'peddling' goods they had made. Local village communities provided most requirements for themselves, the baker making bread, cakes, etc., the farmer and dairyman providing meat, milk, cheese and butter, and from him, the skins would give the cobbler the materials to make shoes, laces, and onto those making clothes from skins, and wool, etc.

By the eighteenth century towns were being established as market towns which enabled the village craftsmen and women to sell the goods they made and to buy materials they needed in their trade. Hotels and Lodging Houses required to buy goods they needed. Gradually the village traders were making regular (perhaps once or twice a week) visits to the market town, and were often asked by those who did not have a horse and cart if they would take and deliver a parcel; buy some goods they needed in the town; and also if they could travel with him in his cart or van. He was becoming a Carrier.

By the early nineteenth century the status of the 'Carrier' was being established evidenced by his inclusion in publications such as Kellys Directory. For those researching local history of that time, these directories provide an invaluable source of information. Divided into separate sections for each village and town, they list all property or business owners; detail local places of interest; and at the heading of each section give the times the post arrives and leaves, and from where; similarly for the Stage Coach, and of equal prominence, the Carrier. Similar to the Stage Coach, they used the local pub or hotel as a base where people could meet, and where their horses could be changed over and rested in stables.

The Carrier's vehicle, horse drawn at this time, but later motor transport from the early 1900s, was usually referred to as a van.

A farm cart, with a canvas cover, and canvas sheets at the front and back to keep out the rain and wind. The passengers would either sit beside the Carrier at the front, or on planks of wood in the back. Children would often sit on the tailboard hanging on chains at the rear of the van, with their legs dangling; many travelled to school on the back of the Carrier's van getting a free lift and avoiding a tiring walk. There was no danger as if the van stopped suddenly you would be thrown up into the van! It was harder to fall off!

The Carriers established regular routes, some travelling on one or two days a week whilst others went every day, and even twice on a Saturday, returning in the evening to allow people to visit the local theatre or place of entertainment. Shops and stalls in the Market area often stayed open until late on Saturday night. Farm workers and other labourers were usually paid on a Saturday, so the Saturday evening trip gave them a chance to enjoy their income. Sadly, most was spent before the next week started. The village would probably have a number of public houses, selling the local brew made in the village brewery, and here too the week's wages would be spent before Saturday night had expired!

With this regular Carrier Service now established, many people who did not have the time to travel, or even do shopping, and wanted to get the Carrier to call at their home, would put a flag outside their home. This signal became a part of the trade, and a common sight in country districts. This is still used to attract tradesmen in some parts of the U.K. into the 21st century, although the Carriers' trade has now mainly ended. The flag could be anything, sometimes a Country's flag or just a piece of cloth or an old bag, on a stick.

Usually there was just one Carrier on a route on any one day, but on busier routes where more than one might pass by, the villagers used differently coloured flags to indicate which one they wanted to call. Some of the better established firms had flags printed with their names on them. Millmore from Ventnor, Ryde and Shanklin; and Chiverton from Ventnor, had printed flags right through until the 1950s.

Some were more imaginative! An elderly lady at Blackgang

used a pair of old ladies' bloomers nailed to a stick as her flag for years. My father claimed that he could name every one of his customers by looking at their flag. No doubt he did this with this lady, but whether he could recognise the flag from its original use I am unable to say.

The effect on the audience for my talk was usually by now the same, as I would put it, a 'little titter' passed among the gathering! I invariably found a female audience responded quicker than a male group. The mention of the flag invariably brought reminiscences from those present. "I remember my grandmother putting out a flag for the Carrier", "My mother had the Carrier call every Friday, we always put out a flag for him to call". I knew then that I had my audience with me!

My father and grandfather had both been Carriers, travelling from Blackgang, through Chale; my grandfather's route going through Shorwell into Newport, until 1916, when his son was called-up for War service and went off to the First World War; and my father went through Chillerton from 1910, when he left school, until he retired in 1964. As a boy I travelled with my father whenever I could.

My publication about Isle of Wight Carriers is entitled "Put Out The Flag" to commemorate the method used by their customers to attract them as they passed along the road.

St. Thomas's Square in Newport was for centuries the official base for all Island Carriers who would travel in from their home villages from all quarters of the Island. Their horses were stabled during the daytime behind the various inns and hotels there. The largest of these was Cockram's Yard behind the Kings Head Inn, where there was room for ten or twelve horses. All the Carriers had a Newport Inn as a base where their passengers could wait for the homeward journey, or leave parcels for collection. Parcels were also left on the road in the middle of the Square, where before 1920 a horse trough stood and where the War Memorial now stands. Parcels brought in from outlying villages for delivery to other parts of the Island would be left for the Carriers from that area to pick up when they arrived. The carriage (6d. or 1/- depending on size) would be left under the string tied round the parcel, and in all the time that I have knowledge of, no money or parcel was ever lost or stolen.

St. Thomas's Square was the hub of activity in the town. Carriers would often take a list of items to a shop, and then call back an hour or two later to pick up the goods; often several parcels for different customers. To help them, up to the Second War, there were old characters, often with a handcart, who would deliver the orders and then collect them later. For this they were given a small payment which was usually spent in the pub. The term 'down and out' could be linked to them.

One such was a Jimmy Puckett, who rarely washed, and spent most of his time swearing about everyone. There was one family of Carriers, the Blakes, Harry, his son Harry, and his son Peter, who ran carriers vans and also small passenger buses around the town. They were always having rows with poor old Jimmy. One day they tied him to his handcart and pushed him down to Sea Street and left him outside the Police Station, where it was then located. No doubt if this happened today, the culprits would be arrested, but on this occasion a Constable left the Station, and noticing the screaming gentleman tied up on his cart, saluted him, said "Good Morning Mr. Puckett" and passed on his way.

There was always great loyalty to their customers, and most Carriers would go beyond the normal call of duty by doing jobs around the home for their customers. One Carrier, Jack Downton from Chale, called at a Mrs. Woodford's home near Shorwell when she left her flag out, and was asked to get her a new toilet seat. Toilets in those days were often in an outside privy and subject to the effects of the weather. She also asked if he would fit it for her when he came back, which he was happy to do (all part of the service). As he went down her path, Mrs. Woodford called out "make sure you get the right size won't you", to which Jack called back "..if you bend over Mrs. Woodford I'll measure your backside and make sure it fits you…". Whether she did I do not know, but she was satisfied with her purchase. This invariably brought another chorus of laughter, particularly from the ladies.

At Brighstone, George Shotter had a larger Carriers business, taking more passengers. This eventually led to the family running coaches, still remembered fondly by many Islanders. He was a highly respected member of the local community and a member of the lifeboat crew. But he always aimed to serve. One winter's evening, delivering parcels in Brighstone and in the dark, with just one lady passenger in the back, he was searching for a parcel when his hand apparently reached inappropriate areas. The lady was heard to say "..you won't find the parcel up there, Mr. Shotter.." but no doubt he found what he was searching for!

The status of Carriers in Victorian times is evidenced by their inclusion in books written by such as Charles Dickens (David Copperfield), and Thomas Hardy. They were as much a part of everyday village life as the baker and the postman.

By early 1900s motor vehicles were replacing horses, but the service was just as popular, and necessary. This also brought competition from companies who provided a passenger service as a priority. One of the best known, which continues to this day, was the Vectis Bus Company (which became the Southern Vectis when they joined with the, then, Southern Railway in the late 1920s). They were able to offer a regular passenger service, and several times a day on each route. One man told me from the 1920s he was able to get to Newport, and return home, before lunchtime, and could get back to work in the afternoon whereas if he used the Carrier a whole day was lost. It was apparently cheaper too, the Carrier charged 2/6d (12p) for a return journey whereas the Vectis charged just 1/6d (7p), but the Carrier did pick you up from, and return you to, your front door.

The Carrier's van was also used for local group outings, with bench seats put in the back to take the passengers. The local Church Sunday School outing, say to Sandown, was a familiar trip in the Carrier's van. I still have those seats!

Some soldiers returning from War became Carriers but needed driving lessons to operate their new service by motor vehicle; although they were fully able to operate with a horse. Vern Barnes from Niton, whose father had been a Carrier, was presented with a new Model T Ford motor van by his mother who had saved 100 sovereigns (£100 in gold) whilst Vern had been away, to set him up in business. My father gave him a driving lesson along

Bleak Down one Saturday afternoon, and that was the only lesson he had, and he later drove heavy goods vehicles. My father had taken on a motor van in 1912 when he left school but found it unreliable, as when it broke down he could not get home. With a horse he could continue on the journey! At one talk I heard one old lady say to her friend, "..I did it along Bleak Down for the first time…", but I don't think she meant driving!

St. Thomas's Square in Newport became busier as the 1920s saw more people becoming Carriers, and by the 1930s the Square became over crowded, and Newport Town Council tried to move them out of their official base. Local businesses and their village customers objected and a petition was drawn up to oppose the Council's plans, and the Council was unable to change matters.

My father's route took him past Whitecroft Hospital, then known as the Lunatic Asylum, where he would call every day to collect or deliver goods. Some of the permanent male patients would provide help unloading the van, and one was quite happy with a piece of Cadbury's chocolate as a reward; but he would not work until he saw that the reward was there. One day it was not, and the only way this patient would allow my father to pass was to show him some chocolate. He found a whole bar of Chocolate Exlax in a customer's bag, and presented this to the helper, who consumed the lot with some glee (he had never had a full bar of chocolate before). Just one small section was enough to do the required job! That afternoon the patient was standing outside the hospital in his best suit. Asking if he was going visiting, he replied that he had the 'diarears'.

Some years later, when he had died, the staff at the hospital were talking about this character, and mentioned the incident to my father and he admitted what he had done. They said the doctors could never find the cause. One nurse there said "..we had to wash him down seven times one day; we ran out of clothes for him!".

Wartime brought in petrol rationing and the Carriers had to restrict their journeys. Local shops who by now were delivering goods in their own vehicles were also restricted (the Carriers did get some extra coupons), and often delivered their goods on alternate days, and used the Carriers on the other days. Some Carriers used bicycles to collect and deliver goods around the town. On one occasion, my father found his bicycle which he had left outside one shop, had been taken. Seeing another bike outside the shop he took that to use. It was some six months or so later when he saw his bike outside a shop and waited to find that Mr. Neat, the Oil Man (and a friend of his) had taken it. They exchanged bikes and remained friends – it was Wartime!

After the War, the Labour Government nationalised public transport and all the larger Carrier firms such as Shepard Brothers; Carter Paterson; Pickfords; Hall and Blann locally, etc. had their carrier trades taken over and they became part of British Road Services, but the smaller, one-man Carriers continued to provide the old service until they retired. Many of the Carriers were by now also providing a furniture removal service.

This was usually the end of my talk, but on one occasion, a lady asked if she could add a comment. I was delighted. She said that her great-great-grandfather had been a Carrier, and he had a special box made, covered in leather, in which he put the dairy produce – milk, butter, cheese, eggs, etc. which he was taking to the market, which was placed in the back of his van. She still had this box, and it has the initials 'I.W.' on the lid. I was thrilled that we had traced a real bit of Isle of Wight carrying history, when she said that he came from Leicestershire, and his name was Ivor Wilkins!!!

(For more details of the old Isle of Wight carrying trade, and names and photographs of many early carriers, see the book "Put Out The Flag" by the author, Derek Sprake.)

CHAPTER 2
The Old Village Show

Written by that great Islander, Jack Lavers, I consider that this short poem gives a true description of how I and many more remember the old village 'Flower Show'. He wrote it about his home village show, Newchurch Show, but it could be about any village show in the period from the early twentieth century to the 1970s.

> Oh, Newchurch Show, OUR Newchurch Show,
> Such memories of long ago.
> The Vicarage field, the crowded tent,
> The parish folk on pleasure bent;
> For all the parish gathered there,
> The great day of the village year,
> AND EVERYONE KNEW EVERYONE,
> With all their news to hear.

And still can be recalled the scent
Of flowers and fruit within the tent,
The huge parsnips, onions, and the peas,
There never were such giants as these!
Carnations, pansies, roses too –
The winners' names were there to view,
AND EVERYONE KNEW EVERYONE,
Old friendships to renew.

Outside the tent, so much to see,
Jim Harden's swings, the tent for tea,
The Skittles with a pig as prize,
The Coconuts on stands for shies,
Brading Band with music gay,
    ('gay' meant something happy in those days!)
The children's races under way,
AND EVERYONE KNEW EVERYONE
To make the perfect day!

Soon after tea the sinking sun
Would smile upon the mile run,
The sack race and the Egg-and-Spoon;
But Show Day ended all too soon
And whether wanting more or no
The time arrived to homeward go,
AND EVERYONE KNEW EVERYONE
"We'll meet at next year's Show"

Oh! Newchurch Show, our Newchurch Show,
What fun it was at Newchurch Show.

Many people told me that those lines brought back so many memories of what village life used to be about. One man told me it was on Show Day that you met your relatives and old friends; often the only day of the year you saw them. People who had moved away from home, or left school, would return to their village on Show Day. It was a day to reminisce; often to introduce your new boyfriend or girlfriend to your relatives or former school friends. A year or two later, to return to show off the new engagement ring, and to be followed by the wedding ring, and a year or so later by a pram with a new baby. Nowadays it is usually the other way round, and then all so often followed by a new boyfriend or girlfriend, and it all repeats itself!

The Village Show was a place to dress in your best clothes; a suit, and a smart dress; indeed the Village Show was looked on rather like a Garden Party, and someone who did not dress-up for the event was regarded as letting the side down. Today, dress is as informal as possible.

But the "Show" for many years was far more important than just a fun day out, it was the event which might ensure your employment for the next year. The earliest shows on the Island started around 1860, a time when there were many large houses with extensive gardens, all employing gardeners, under-gardeners, jobbing gardeners, and other staff to maintain the grounds. Each garden had to provide the house with both vegetables for the table and flowers of all kinds for decorating the home, and the Head Gardener's job might well depend on his success in the local show. If he was beaten by a neighbour's gardener he might well lose his job, so he would do everything, both legal and not, to ensure he won! It was not unknown for exhibits from one home where a relative of the gardener was a gardener, sometimes from a mainland garden, would find their way to the other garden, just before show day. My father was a Carrier, and for some years in the 1920s a day or so before Chale Show, a large hamper would arrive at Newport Railway Station destined for a man who was the Head Gardener of a local house. That gardener was usually very successful at the following Show! One year the lid of the hamper 'accidentally' came open, only to reveal a selection of the highest quality root vegetables (carrots, parsnips, and potatoes) and peas and beans, etc.

The local Show was always reported at length by the local press, as evidenced by an article in the Isle of Wight Times (the Ryde paper of the time) in 1863 of the Royal Isle of Wight Horticultural Society's Annual Show. The "Royal" title was evidence of the great support Queen Victoria gave to Isle of Wight Shows. Newspapers rarely had photographs before the Second World War, so the expertise of the journalist to describe the event in words was skillfully used as these extracts demonstrate:-

"The Show was one of the very best that has been seen in Ryde for years; the fuschias, geraniums and begonias, well blossomed and fine coloured, while the ornamental foliaged plants were almost as variegated in hue as their more gaily blossoming neighbours; the ferns and mosses, in their modest attire, were as attractive as anything in the show. The cut flowers were very fine, and Col. Harcourt, in mixed blooms and roses, carried off the palm (main award) as usual. The fruit and cucumbers were quite up to the mark. The six orchard-house trees exhibited by Mr. Colenutt deserve especial notice for their fruitfulness and beauty."

The expert displays by the professional gardeners were complimented by a reference to the lower class – "The Cottagers devices in wild flowers call for special commendation".

The whole event was described:-

"It was a lovely day and the Company, (visitors) as usual, was composed of the *elite* of Ryde and the vicinity, and it would be no 'fancy sketch' to say, that when the beautiful grounds were thickly studded with youth and beauty arrayed in gay costumes, and the splendid band of the 55th regiment was filling the air with its thrilling harmony, that the grounds of Buckingham Villa presented a most enchanting scene."

There followed a full list of winners in each class, the majority with the name of their gardener given.

Those early Shows were usually held in the extensive grounds of a 'large' house which in itself added to that property's standing. At Freshwater, Alfred Lord Tennyson provided Farringford House, as did his successors, until 1939.

The reference to 'Cottagers' in the report above raises an interesting division of how shows used to be staged. In Chale we had separate classes for Gardeners (professionals who earned their living from working in gardens), Amateurs, home owners (people who did not earn their living from gardening), and Cottagers. For many years I did not know what the difference was, but having seen schedules for Freshwater Show in 1926, the mystery was solved. A cottager was a person who lived in a rented 'cottage' often 'tied' to the job in which he was employed (a farm worker would have lived in a cottage which went with his job, and when he lost his job for whatever reason, he lost his house as well. Or if he changed employers he would move house to another 'tied' to his new job). Indeed, at Freshwater a cottager's house must not have a rent of more than £20 per annum, inclusive of rates and taxes, and that's about 39p a week!

It would appear that even with such clear indications, some tried to evade the rules for in 1927 the description of a cottager was further clarified "…he must be a bona fide working man, in receipt of a weekly wage, whose garden is cultivated in his leisure time, and who has not employed extra labour for his garden in any way." So there!

I have been fortunate to be provided with schedules (lists of show classes) for some early shows. Niton & Whitwell had their first show in 1865, and in 1873 their schedule shows Cottagers as 'Common Labourers'. However, the classes were not dissimilar to those we might see for today's shows:- fruit - Apples, Pears and Plums; flowers – Dahlias, Asters, Fuschias and Petunias, and vegetables – Potatoes, Carrots, Onions, Beans and Peas, etc. However, it is the numbers of each exhibit which used to be much greater than we see in today's shows. 12 potatoes in each dish, 9 parsnips, 12 onions, 30 pods of beans or peas, but still 2 cabbages and 2 lettuces.

To go to those early shows was quite costly. In 1873 at Niton it cost 1/- all afternoon, or just 6d after 4 o'clock. In another schedule for Brighstone Show in 1901, the cost was 1/- at the gate; although it was cheaper if you bought a ticket during the days before. I compare this to a farm labourer's wages of the time of probably 6/- or 7/- a week. (The village show was always expensive to put on, and prizes were awarded to winning exhibitors.)

In many of the early shows, it was not just individual exhibits which were presented for competition, but beds of plants or whole gardens judged against others.

At Niton, in 1873, there were prizes of 5/- for the best Kitchen

Garden, and best Flower Garden. At Brighstone, Beds of Onions, and Plants in Pots had to be entered nearly 2 months before show day, and they would be open for judging shortly after they were entered.

In Chale in 1935, Mrs. Priestley, the first wife of the well-known author and broadcaster Mr. J.B. Priestley, who lived at Billingham Manor, offered £5 for the best flower garden. Mrs. Priestley requested that the prize money should be spread amongst a number of exhibitors to encourage as many as possible to grow flowers.

Right up to the 1930s, the Rt. Hon. Lord Tennyson was giving a special prize for the best kept and cultivated allotment in Freshwater.

The Brighstone schedule of 1901 lists in its Rules "…all exhibits should be brought to the tents as soon as possible after 8.00 a.m. on the day of the show; none will be allowed in after 11.00 a.m. except for boiled potatoes…".

Now that raises an interesting part of all shows. There are some things which need special consideration. Even today, roses should be judged before other exhibits, as in a warm tent the blooms will quickly open, and this ensures the judge will see the rose as the exhibitor intended! Boiled spuds is another such. What happens to a boiled potato left in the air? – it will go 'black'! So, boiled potatoes were always allowed in 'late', and would be judged as soon as they were exhibited.

In giving this talk, it is the condition of boiled potatoes which produces more comments from the audience than any. One lady told me she would put a piece of (clean – washed) coal in with her potatoes whilst they were being boiled. Several other ladies said their mothers used to do the same. Others disagreed! But all agreed they would go black if left in the air. Another lady said she arrived at her show at the allotted time, and there were six or seven ladies all running over to the tent door carrying bowls of steaming boiled potatoes. As she got to the door of the tent, she tripped over the tent peg, and her potatoes went all over the ground. There being no time to return home and boil more, she said she picked them up, dusted them off, and put them back in the bowl and so into the show. She won FIRST PRIZE. It just shows you should never give up!

My home village of Chale now stages the largest event on the Island, and a magnificent two-day event it is, and whilst it incorporates the origins of a village show it lacks the intimate nature of the Old Village Show much loved by the old village communities.

Whereas many shows started in the mid-1800s, Chale did not have a Vegetable and Flower Show until 1920. Many village events took place earlier, mainly under the general heading of 'Sports', and the Village Show had involved sports, and still does.

Around the start of the 20th century fierce competition took place between Chale and Niton, particularly with an annual Tug-of-War event. At one time the newly appointed Rector of Niton was persuaded to be the coach for the Niton team. He had found his popularity was not high and was somewhat reluctant to take on the role. When his team lost, he thought that was the end, and at the following Sunday service he feared the worst, but instead of rejection, he found the Church full and everyone was thrilled that he had taken on the challenge, determined to win next year!

Other events followed, and in 1909, 1910 and 1911 a Chale Regatta was held on the shore at Blackgang, under Blackgang Chine. Various swimming, rowing and sailing events took place between the village residents. They even had a Dogs' Race – the dogs were taken out into the sea in boats and (albeit a relatively short distance off shore) thrown overboard into the sea and encouraged by their owners standing on the beach, swam home to tumultuous applause!

By 1914 a full programme of athletic sports was held in a field which was to become the home for Chale Show after the War. Races for children, even a babies' race for the under 5s, was followed by a variety of events including Pole Jump, Long Jump, Hurdle races, etc. A Pole and Bolster Contest involved people sitting on a pole and knocking each other off with a bolster (a long pillow) thrown at the opponent's head or body. This stayed popular until into the late 1900s. (Before Health and Safety ruled our lives!) A Ladies' Egg and Spoon race (still held) and an Amusement Race for Ladies where the competitors put on items of clothing from piles every few yards. Why was there no Amusement Race for Men?, but as one person commented, the Amusement Race for Ladies WAS the amusement race for men!

The day ended with a Tug-of-War between men who lived on either side of the road in Chale. A Tug-of-War was also a popular event for many years.

It was significant that the programme states 'No entrance fee and no gate money', and yet prize money was awarded. Indeed, Chale Show was always a 'free' event until around 1980; so how was this possible? Well, there was always a house-to-house collection before the event each year and the money collected usually covered costs, and as 'everyone' who lived in Chale had made a payment, they went to the Show for free, and just so that everyone knew what had been paid – there was no set amount, it was a donation; the names of everyone and how much they had given was printed in the Show schedule every year. When these were delivered, the first thing villagers did was to see how much each person had paid, particularly any new resident. There was an unofficial 'rate'. The wealthy landowners probably donated a £1 or a Guinea (remember this started before the First World War), businessmen would give 10/- or ½ Guinea; retired landowners say 5/-, families 2/6d, and single people 2/- or 1/6d. If you could not afford this you put in 6d so your name showed on the schedule list of donors!

People were giving similar amounts right up to the 1970s. It came to an end when it was noted that one collector had entered less than he had been given on the schedule list!!

On Saturday, July 19th 1919 'Chale Peace Sports' were held in the field opposite The Rectory. There was a Tug-of-War with teams of Service and Ex-service Men v. Civilians. After similar sports to those held in 1914, there was a children's tea followed by adults' tea and a 'Short United Religious Service' on the field. The evening ended with a bonfire at 11.00 p.m. A copy of the Sports Programme appears at the end of this chapter.

As said, the Sports Committee started a Show after the First World War and introduced a Cottage Garden Show on Thursday,

3rd August 1920, and the Show was always held on a Thursday (all village shows were held on the date when the nearest town had its early closing day – Newport, Thursday. Godshill Show on a Wednesday, as Ventnor's early closing day; Brighstone on a Thursday because of Newport being on the Thursday). The full title was 'Cottage Garden Show & Sports for Chale postal and school area'. The president was always the Rector (Rev. C.W. Heald in 1920), and the officers made up of village businessmen. The show was held in a field at Bramstone, kindly lent by Mr. S. Cheek, farmer.

Classes were not dissimilar to those for Niton show before, but there was one special prize (Cups came later). The overall winner received 'A Superb Large-sized Solid Bronze Plaque, specially designed as a Show-Championship Award by Sir Hamo Thornycroft, R.A., and portraying a beautiful female figure engaged in gardening work' and presented by Toogood, the Southampton Seedsmen; and also a 'Toogood Certificate of Excellence in Horticulture'. I had one of these Certificates in my stores, but not one of the bronze plaques (and I really wanted to see what a beautiful female figure engaged in gardening work looked like!!) After asking around for well over a year I was eventually presented with one, which I treasure. All I can say is that the description has some poetic license! (Beauty is in the eye of the beholder.) A description of one exhibitor's entries to this first show can be seen in 'Men of Chale' by the author. The Show was clearly a great success, and still goes on today.

It was not until 1926 that a Horticultural Society was formed and took over running the old Chale Show from the Sports Committee.

One can get so much information from old Minute Books, and one or two items from those early books for Chale are mentioned here.

For many years Chale Show gave a prize of ½ cwt artificial manure (donated by SCATS, now Mole Valley of Blackwater), but the first such prize was ½ cwt Bone Manure given by their predecessors, the I.W. Farmers Trading Society. The Minute reads – "… it was decided at a General Meeting held on the Show field on 31st July 1934 to award the Bone Manure to the Exhibitor having the most entries and the fewest prizes, and it was unanimously agreed to present the Bone Manure to Mr. Wiggins, as he had qualified for same, viz. 5 entries and no prizes. Runner up was Mr. S. Cheek (Snr.) with 7 entries and 1 prize. (He was mad as anything because if he had not won the prize he would have got the Bone Manure!)

In 1935 it was Minuted that "...in order to encourage the cultivation of Flower Gardens in the District, Mrs. Priestly of Billingham had generously offered £5" etc. as previously noted.

Disaster struck in 1937 when the Secretary had to inform members that, in paying out the prize money at the Scouts Hall on Saturday, 7th August, someone, he could not state definitely who, had asked for and taken prize money of 3/- in a pay envelope awarded to Miss Sylvia Whittington at the Annual Show, and up to last Monday, 11th October, Miss Whittington had not received the money. The Secretary had paid that amount (3/-) to Mr. L. Whittington on 13th October from his own finances.

A poignant item was recorded, and headed as Final Meeting held in Feb. 1940 "...Proposed by Mr. Eede and seconded by Mr. H. Chiverton that no more Shows be held for the duration of the War". The Minutes were signed as correct on 24th September 1945 by the Chairman, Mr. Fred Mew. It is interesting that in the depths of the start of the War there was faith that the War would eventually end and life would return to some normality, but did they think it would take five and a half years!

In the context of "The Old Village Show", the period between the two Wars was very important. Villages took part in many horticultural displays. Photographs of many magnificent displays still exist, put on by gardeners from Chale, and many other villages, at exhibitions by such as the "Isle of Wight Horticultural Association's Great Autumn Fruit & Vegetable Exhibition for the encouragement of food production on the Isle of Wight." I have one such certificate for 1927, and magnificent it is too.

Other types of celebration were coronation festivities, such as at Gatcombe as shown in Brian Greening's excellent publication 'One Hundred Years before the Mast'. Prizes in children's races included a cane-handled cricket bat, an Aero-Revolver, and a whistle for boys 10 to 13 years; a writing desk, a brass inkstand and a mouth organ for High Jump for Boys under 15 years; and for Egg & Spoon, a silver brooch, a pair of vases, and a mouth organ for girls under 12 years. Adults received even more useful tools as prizes including a prong, an axe, and a kettle in Pole Jump; and a spade, a watering can, and a hammer in 'Othagon' Open (and if you know what an Othagon was, please let me know!).

The same book contains pictures of Chale Sports where the hurdle race is over sheep hurdles (the true meaning of the word).

The village sports were not only fun, but provided fierce competition for most young men, indeed some went on to higher athletic prowess, and even national, and Olympic success. The village sports were an important part of athletic training.

It was not always so serious, and anyone could take part. One man at Chale in the early days entered a running race, but not having the right gear, took off his trousers and ran round the course in his 'long-johns'. His wife, being embarrassed at seeing her husband's lack of attire, ran after him waving his trousers, shouting at him to put his trousers on; a sight which provided a major amusing talking point for weeks to come.

I have a programme from Brighstone Athletic Sports of 1928 with prizes of a manicure set, a fountain pen, and a pencil on a stand for a girls' race for under 10s; and for girls under 16, an ebony clock, a box manicure, and a comb in a case! The adults' races were held under AAA rules and prizes were given, donated by businesses in Newport – sponsorship in the 1920s. These included a case of stainless steel knives: a coffee pot, and a copper kettle for the ½ Mile Race; and a set of carvers, an inkstand, and a condiment set for the One Mile Race. My father won some of these prizes, and I still have them to this day!

Other events included the Wheel Barrow Race; Pole & Bolster; Tilting the Bucket; and the Greasy Pole. Competitors came from all over the Island to take part.

You may recall that in the Wheel Barrow Race, two people took part with one holding the other's legs whilst the other one 'walked' with their hands on the ground. One lady told me at one 'talk' that when she was young, she went in for the Wheel Barrow Race with a friend. Whilst she was 'athletic', the friend was, well, not. They started off with the athletic girl 'on the ground' and were leading at half way, when the rules stated they had to change over. By the time they reached the finishing line, they finished after the following race had ended, and everyone cheered for their effort!

A Tug-of-War competition took place all afternoon, with the final the last event of the day, by which time it was almost dark. There were also Side-Shows with Skittles with the traditional live pig for the winner. Almost everyone who lived in the country in those days kept a pig at the bottom of the garden; it ate all food waste from the house and garden, and provided pork or bacon for the house when fat enough; nothing was wasted in those days. There was a Guessing the Weight of a Lump of Coal side-show with the prize 5 cwt of coal – well worth winning; and an additional competition of Clues with the prize given by the Vectis Bus Coy.

During the course of giving this talk, I have been provided with many stories from the audience.

One elderly lady said her father had been the policeman at St. Helen's before the First World War. Her mother entered a sponge cake in the Show, and won first prize. However, on going to collect her cake at the end of the day she found it had been knocked onto the ground and a boot had been stamped on it; policemen were not popular in those days.

A lady said she and her new husband had to live with her mother-in-law when they first got married; they did not get on! She was no good at cooking, but when she came in on the evening before their local Show, her husband congratulated her on the cooking of some lovely small cakes. He had found them in a tin on the kitchen table. "They are your mother's ready for the Show". Not knowing what to do, and fearing they would be kicked out if the mother found out what had happened, she said she went down to the Co-op and bought some cake mixture and made some more. The end of the story was that they had to leave the following Saturday!

Another lady, who was a Young Farmer, said she had made a fruit cake some time before their Annual Show, and put it in a tin in a cupboard. When she went to get it out for the event she found a large wedge had been cut out, and yes, her husband admitted it was he who had enjoyed the meal!

My mother enjoyed great success with sponge cakes at several Shows. One of her inherited cousins remarked to her at Chale Show that she "was lucky again". "Luck", she replied, "it was skill!"

Some gardeners would do anything to gain that extra point to win a Cup. One judge, on finding the 'colour' came off some potatoes, found they had had boot polish applied to turn some white 'spuds' into coloured ones.

One man (no names) who lived at Chale always won first prize for his cucumbers. Every year, on the Tuesday before Chale Show on the Thursday, he would go by bus, with what he called "mother's shopping bag" into the Covent Garden Market in Newport where vegetables were sold by auction, mainly to hotels and guest houses and the like. Village people could send their surplus vegetables into the market, and there was no waste. This old chap would select two of the very best, identical, cucumbers, with a nice flower on the end. He would pay the auctioneer and place them in mother's bag and leave it in the Office at the back of the Auction Rooms. He would then walk round to St. Thomas's Square and ask my father, the Chale Carrier, to collect the bag and deliver it to his home, as usual. It would be delivered that evening.

The following day, he would invite any passing person who he knew would be going to the Show, to inspect his wonderful pair of cucumbers which were in his frame, amongst a fine array of green leaves. "They be fer Show…" but they were not actually attached to the plants. If anyone doubted their authenticity the following day when he had won the first prize, he would get the friend who had seen them the day before to confirm that they had indeed come from his garden!

This old chap used to wheel his exhibits to the show in a wheelbarrow, with his prize cucumbers sitting on the top. One year around 1950, he had not arrived as judging time approached. Yes, he had been seen leaving his house that morning with his exhibits as usual, so where was he? A search party was sent out, across the show field, down the lane to the road where his wife was seen running up the road. She shouted "Wait, wait, Jack's coming". Someone asked where he was, fearing he might have been taken ill when she said "He's behind the hedge having a shite!" He eventually arrived and set up his exhibits, but it is the only time I ever heard of a Show being held up for a convenience! (That is the point where I always sat down, usually to broad laughter.)

Some years before I had always included that story in the middle of my talk about Old Village Shows. However, one evening after a talk to a ladies group, a lady telephoned and asked if I would give the talk to her group. Of course I said "Yes". "There is just one request, please will you put the 'Shite' story last". I did and ever since found that was always the perfect ending to this particular talk!

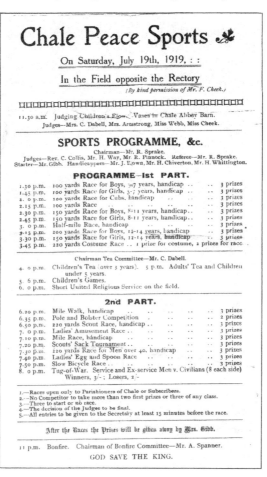

Chale Peace Sports

On Saturday, July 19th, 1919, : :

In the Field opposite the Rectory

(By kind permission of Mr. F. Cheek.)

11.30 a.m.   Judging Children's Flow . Vases in Chale Abbey Barn.
Judges—Mrs. C. Dabell, Mrs. Armstrong, Miss Webb, Miss Cheek.

SPORTS PROGRAMME, &c.

Chairman—Mr. R. Sprake.
Judges—Rev. C. Collis, Mr. H. Way, Mr. R. Pinnock.   Referee—Mr. R. Sprake.
Starter—Mr. Gibb.   Handicappers—Mr. J. Eown, Mr. H. Chiverton, Mr. H. Whittington.

PROGRAMME—1st PART.

1.30 p.m.	100 yards Race for Boys, 7 years, handicap	3 prizes
1.45 p.m.	100 yards Race for Girls, 5-7 years, handicap	3 prizes
2. 0 p.m.	100 yards Race for Cubs, handicap	3 prizes
2.15 p.m.	100 yards Race	3 prizes
2.30 p.m.	150 yards Race for Boys, 8-11 years, handicap..	3 prizes
2.45 p.m.	150 yards Race for Girls, 8-11 years, handicap..	3 prizes
3. 0 p.m.	Half-mile Race, handicap	3 prizes
3.15 p.m.	200 yards Race for Boys, 12-14 years, handicap	3 prizes
3.30 p.m.	150 yards Race for Girls, 12-14 years, handicap ..	3 prizes
3.45 p.m.	220 yards Costume Race .. 1 prize for costume, 2 prizes for race .

Chairman Tea Committee—Mr. C. Dabell.

4. 0 p.m.	Children's Tea (over 5 years). 5 p.m. Adults' Tea and Children under 5 years.
5. 6 p.m.	Children's Games.
6. 0 p.m.	Short United Religious Service on the field.

2nd PART.

6.20 p.m.	Mile Walk, handicap	3 prizes
6.35 p.m.	Pole and Bolster Competition	2 prizes
6.50 p.m.	220 yards Scout Race, handicap	3 prizes
7. 0 p.m.	Ladies' Amusement Race	3 prizes
7.10 p.m.	Mile Race, handicap	3 prizes
7.20 p.m.	Scouts' Sack Tournament	3 prizes
7.30 p.m.	220 yards Race for Men over 40, handicap ..	3 prizes
7.40 p.m.	Ladies' Egg and Spoon Race	3 prizes
7.50 p.m.	Slow Bicycle Race	3 prizes
8. 0 p.m.	Tug-of-War. Service and Ex-service Men v. Civilians (8 each side) Winners, 3/-; Losers, 2/-

1.—Races open only to Parishioners of Chale or Subscribers.
2.—No Competitor to take more than two first prizes or three of any class.
3.—Three to start or no race.
4.—The decision of the Judges to be final.
5.—All entries to be given to the Secretary at least 15 minutes before the race.

After the Races the Prizes will be given away by Mrs. Gibb.

11 p.m.   Bonfire.   Chairman of Bonfire Committee—Mr. A. Spanner.
GOD SAVE THE KING.

CHAPTER 3
The Funny Side of Banking

It is difficult to accept in the early parts of the 21st century that there could be a 'funny' side of banking. The banking industry is in such a total mess, it is an embarrassment to admit that one once worked in an industry which has caused so much trouble for our Nation. But there it is, and I did indeed work for a Bank all my employed life, until I took early retirement when still just 50 years old, and now they pay my pension (I hope!). I do not say their name. (So I hold up a carrier bag resplendent with the National Westminster Bank name and logo.) So be it!

During my time with what was always known as 'the Bank', firstly Nat. Prov., I acquired the odd relic which, without my forethought would have been lost forever! The word is not 'steal', rather 'retain'!

I have a selection of old bank money boxes, usually used to promote small savings accounts for children, probably the best known of which were the 'NatWest Piggies'. Each had an individual name, mainly modelled on a prominent character of the 1980s. My example is of a portly (pig) gentleman with blue trousers and a red and white tie. The audience is asked to name him at the end. One such pig was named after Margaret Thatcher, dressed in blue, who was quite well known at the time! (Children got the first, Woody, when they opened the account, and then the next piggy for every £50 they saved in the account, collecting 5 in all, which have in themselves gained some value these days.)

I produce other money boxes which were issued for savings accounts in earlier years. One in the middle part of the 20th century was in the form of a book with the title 'An aid to thrift' and was issued by the National Provincial Bank, and similar types by other Banks. In Victorian times a solid metal box was issued. They had a slot for coins and a small hole for notes. Each of these could only be opened with a key kept by the Bank cashier. In my experience the cashier could never find the key when the box was brought in by a young customer, who would burst into tears because they wanted their money. The cashier would try to placate the screaming child by breaking open the box with a screwdriver, making it unusable again, which resulted in a fresh burst of tears!

Banknotes issued by the former 'Newport, Isle of Wight Bank' (for £10, in 1788) and by the former 'Isle of Wight Bank' (also £10, in 1802) which form part of my acquired collection are usually handed round (which keeps the audience occupied for a few minutes!). Another item given to me by a former customer is a paid cheque drawn on the London County & Westminster Bank Ltd. for £5 on 10th August 1914 and payable to The Prince of Wales. At one time customers' 'paid cheques' were returned to them with their statements. Cheques also had to be endorsed by the payee before being paid into the Bank. This, sadly, only has a rubber stamp saying 'per pro HIS ROYAL HIGHNESS THE PRINCE OF WALES' and is signed by an equerry! It is assumed the cheque was a donation to a Trust started by the future King

Edward VIII towards the Great War effort. £5 was a considerable sum in 1914.

I also have several examples of bank passbooks issued before typed or computer produced statements became normal. Early passbooks and statements always had overdrawn balances shown in red – the reason for the expression 'being in the red'. When this stopped with computer statements, which could not print in different colours, many customers claimed that because an overdrawn balance was printed in black (in the black) they were not actually overdrawn!

Passbooks were handwritten on paper, bound in books, with covers in velum, and the best handwriting had to be used. I believe the only handwritten passbooks used in the 21st century are for Her Majesty the Queen's private bank accounts.

The earliest passbook I have is issued by Birkbeck Bank, a single branch bank where transactions were made by post. Printed and dated 1886, the Manager was a Francis Ravenscroft. In the printed instructions in the book it states that "…Coin and Bank Notes should be sent in Registered Letters. In the case of a Bank Note, the safest plan is to cut it in half, forwarding the first half, and retaining the second until receipt of the first is made known…". One lady told me that she recalled seeing her grandmother, in 1915, sitting at the table, cutting her Bank Notes in half. She thought she had gone mad, but now realised she was just sending them to her Bank.

Bank Notes in Victorian times were rare and only of the highest value. There were gold sovereigns up to £5 in value, so the notes being cut in half were of a higher value than £5.

When this country gave up the Gold Standard in 1931, paper 'notes' were issued for all values; 10/- and £1 by The Treasury, and £5 and above by the Bank of England. Gold sovereigns are, however, still issued for most years, to the present day. Older Bank cashiers always referred to the smaller value notes as just notes, and £5 notes as Bank Notes.

Another item which I rescued from a skip (or worse) in Newport was a battered hardback book with a lock. With lettered 'index' pages at the front and with blotting paper inserts, the other pages are numbered and made up of tissue paper, on which are copied letters written by the Manager, and date from 1876. The earliest are in handwritten script. This was the Manager's confidential letter book in which he would record, under lock, those letters which he would not wish seen by members of his staff.

These letters present an example of what life was like in those days, and how different to modern times.

Earliest letters refer mainly to the 'premises', the building which formed the Bank offices. On 14th September 1878 the Manager who had clearly only arrived shortly before, wrote to 'Head Office', addressing them as 'Gentlemen' seeking sanction "…to spend £3.10.0 as per the enclosed estimate, for cleaning and painting the front of our premises, as our next door neighbour is now engaged upon his". Thinking the Gentlemen in London might not know what his premises looked like, he enclosed a photograph (using the new technology of the day) and wrote "…you will observe that we possess an excellent frontage in the 'Market Square' (St. James Square, where the cattle market was held on Saturdays, and later on Tuesdays), though our working space is so limited that I can only work at one end of the counter when in the office, and our safe arrangements are so very small and insecure that we frequently have to leave larger boxes and other valuables from the safe, in the office not having sufficient room to get them in our strong room…".

On 29th April 1879 he wrote again. "…I beg to re-open this question and state the great need existing for an alteration in our present premises".

"For a staff of seven the office is very small with the oldest possible fittings and the safe accommodation most deplorable, and totally inadequate to the safe keeping of our customers' securities.

"The House is very old necessitating frequent trivial repairs, and overrun both upstairs and down with Beetles of prodigious size…" (presumably Cockroaches?).

Several letters pass between both offices in the following months, and by November 1879 work has started. The Manager had at first refused to move out of his home, the flat above the office which was traditionally the 'tied house' for all Bank Managers. On 11th November 1879 he wrote, "It is totally untrue that the Contractors have been delayed for 17 clear days owing to my still being in the house; on the contrary, the workmen have been fully occupied up to the present since they first commenced on Monday 31st instant, and I have myself let the workmen in, at 6 o'clock in the morning, and I have caught a fearful cold in the consequence. Had H.O. replied to my letters about a month ago on the subject, I was prepared then to vacate.

I am dear Sir, yours faithfully, ...".

Again in 1877, correspondence indicated the then Manager was under some stress himself. Managers were judged for promotion on how they presented their reports, and the following excerpts from letters to H.O. indicate that he was having problems! He wrote – "…and I thank you for being so good as to fill in the form for me… I assure you it is farthest from my wishes to forward you any reports in a slovenly or incorrect manner". (Clearly repeating their words to him!) The next day, he wrote again –

"I did firstly reject the request to lend him the money, but he pressed me to apply for the Director's permission, that, to get rid of him I consented to do so thinking that you would write him such a letter that I could show it to him".

and then ….

"Gentlemen, If I continue to receive letters from you like the ones sent to me lately, I shall certainly lose all moral courage and have to apply for the Directors' considerations, as such communications quite upset me and incapacitate me for my duties."

On 18th November 1878 the Manager wrote to H.O. saying he would be in London the next day to acquaint Head Office of a serious incident at the Capital & Counties Bank (later Lloyds) in Ventnor. The matter soon became of great public interest, and a full account appeared in the Isle of Wight Express of Tuesday, 3rd December 1878 (a local Island Newspaper); a copy being provided by Fay Brown of the Ventnor Historical Society.

The Manager at the Capital & Counties Bank was a Mr. Richard King who had held the position for some 16 or so years. He had been in the habit of writing up customers' accounts and passbooks, and several cheques ranging from a few hundred pounds to two thousand pounds had fraudulently been placed to some customers' accounts who had become overdrawn for large sums, and his own. Mr. King had shown them in the correct customers' passbooks, but not in their accounts in the Bank's books! Several well known farmers and butchers had been involved. Mr. King and his wife had disappeared and were thought to have gone to Spain! The chief clerk, a Mr. Coward, was also involved, and the matter was now in the hands of the Police. The whole matter had a derogatory effect on Ventnor, and the trade of the whole Island. King had gone to Buenos Aires where he apparently turned to drink, but avoided prosecution!

From 1914, most of the letters related to staff, who in the main, had 'been naughty!!'. On 8th April 1914, it was reported that, W.B. Head, a Clerk, had "…fallen into intemperate habits to some extent. His work is still done satisfactorily and we have nothing to complain of, but his personal habits have deteriorated during the last two months…. ".

Up until the start of the Great War, it was rare for ladies to work in a Bank, but as more and more young men were called up for War duties, Banks had to take on lady staff for basic clerical duties, but at a lower salary than was paid for men. During the War the proportion of men to ladies changed dramatically. Some young men joining the staff did not come up to expectations.

The following extracts are from a long letter sent on 11th June 1919 to Head Office. "W.J. Murch. I beg to enclose for your perusal and return a letter which this youth has written to a 'Turn' at one of the local cinemas.

"When this youth first came here I noticed, at once, that he suffered from a lack of concentration of thought when spoken to and became at once apparently tongue-tied and unable to answer the question put to him, for some minutes. This, I put down to extreme nervousness, but I am afraid it can, in my opinion, now only be attributed to either excessive overstudy or a slight mental derangement. …one of my clerks taking a walk in the suburbs of the town (Newport!) found a County Council election notice had had the name of the prospective candidate crossed out, and

W.J. Murch, K.C., M.P. substituted. He at first denied having done this, but subsequently admitted it, regarding it as a joke.

"He studied for his Bankers Examination up to all hours in the morning, which I have put a stop to and ordered that he must not read after 10.30pm. He has, however, got the better of me over this by getting up early in the morning and doing it. I feel he should be moved to somewhere nearer his parents.…".

14th October 1921. To another branch.

"I am prepared to release Mr. Adames in exchange for a capable Lady Clerk (an adding machine would be of small use to us here)…"

29th March 1922. To another branch.

"Head Office are sending one of my youngsters to you, to wit, Mr. Gammon. You will find him a very nice boy. He knows quite a lot, and is most willing and attentive. Unfortunately he is on the small side, so that you two will be a very good 'set off' to each other. …"

4th October 1922. To Staff Department.

"A local Solicitor has been to see me to recommend a youth for our staff. He, Raymond de Banfer Guyon, is 18 years of age, and the son of the late Capt. Guyon, at one time Governor of Parkhurst Prison. His Mother is also dead!

"He is 5'8" and I am told most suitable in every way for our employ." (Remember that, most suitable in every way…). "He has been educated at Cheltenham College" (they took boys as well as girls) "but he could not attain the necessary standard of learning for his age, as he is slow, but thorough." (Clearly very suitable to work in a Bank!)

"He has been fruit farming for a year, but does not like it, and is much more suitable for office life. He has a private income of £100 a year and comes into more money when he attains his majority. He is at present living with an elder brother who is slightly mentally defective, but I am assured there is nothing whatever wrong with this boy. The sister is going to London to take a degree, with a view to earning her own living. She also has a private income."

(and then there is the punchline!)

"There is an Uncle, Mr. McDonald who is nearly a millionaire, but he will have nothing to do with this side of the family owing to having quarrelled with the mother – but that does not follow that he never will." (This Manager would quite like to have a millionaire as a customer, and a millionaire in 1922 was a millionaire!) (Could this Mr. McDonald have made his fortune by selling beef burgers?) "There is no doubt but that this boy is just the type we want.

"Shall I see you at the Managers' Dinner?"

29th February 1924. To another branch.

"I am asked to take young …. on my staff. …. I shall be obliged if you will tell me what you have up against him? Is he careless, and wants the fear of God put into him, or what? Anything you can tell me I shall not use in evidence against him of course, but the information will be useful!"

9th December 1925. To Staff Department.

(A footnote in handwriting ..)

"I will take another lady if you have a good one…" (!)

23rd November 1933. To Staff Department.

"Headed – Clerk (named) Short in postages £2.

"This Clerk came to me to say he had something unfortunate to tell me. He informed me he was £2 short in his postages.

"I interviewed him and elicitated the following information. On the morning of the 15th instant he drew £2 with which to replenish his postages. He went to the Post Office to get the stamps, but, on putting his hand in his pocket, discovered he was minus the £2. I asked him which pocket he put the notes in and his reply was one of his side trouser pockets, he did not remember which. I then asked him how he could have lost them out of his pocket and he replied that he had a large hole in each. He said he kept his loose cash in his hip pocket.

"I asked him why he had not previously reported the loss and his reply was that he was afraid to as he had 'the wind up'.... ".

- -

At this point the book had stopped being used, no doubt a new filing system was introduced!

I now revert to my own reminiscences!

When I first went to Ventnor I was greeted by a distinguished local Doctor, Dr. Williamson, who on seeing my name on the counter remarked "Sprake, Sprake. Do you come from Chale?" I replied "Yes, Sir". The Doctor replied, "Biggest rogues on the Isle of Wight". A good start in a new branch; he was referring to our families' association with the smuggling trade!

Accident Book – An accident book has to be kept where staff are employed to record any incident which might lead to an insurance claim. The first entry in the book at one branch referred to an accident with a lady; the cause in the appropriate column was 'Fell off toilet seat whilst positioning herself' (...but it did not say what position she was attempting).

First Aid Box – Having fixed a new First Aid Box in an appropriate position on the wall, the Manager, whilst explaining its use to his staff, dropped some papers on the floor. He bent down and in picking them up hit his head on the box and had to go to hospital and have six stitches applied!

Fainting – Whilst many people feel like fainting when looking at their balance, one lady had (sadly) a habit of fainting every time she came into the Bank. We later found that she did so in almost every shop she went into! The first time she approached the cashier, and turning completely 'grey', fell onto the floor in the public space. Our first reaction was to administer 'First-Aid', and to 'keep her warm' with a blanket. There being no blanket readily at hand, a Union Jack flag was produced and laid over the poor casualty with her head showing at one end, and her feet at the other. An elderly gentleman of military appearance, on seeing the flag, saluted and left the branch! After this, the same thing happened quite regularly. A few seconds later she would recover, and get up unaware of what had happened; we would simply leave her on the floor for a short time and allow her to arise in her own good time.

This was sometimes of concern to a customer. A foreign student, cashing some travellers cheques witnessed the incident one day, and tapping on the glass to attract the attention of the cashier, said in broken English – "...lady dead on floor". The cashier simply replied "That's OK, she often does that". Fearing she had got her English wrong, the student said "No, lady has died on floor", to which the cashier replied again "Don't worry, she will get up". On doing so, the student ran out of the Bank, never to be seen again!

On being transferred to Ventnor in the 1960s, it was explained that one of my duties was to make the tea, and specifically for the Manager who had his own special cup and saucer, etc. on a tray. The use of tea leaves, and a strainer, were explained to me. After having taken the tea into the Manager the next afternoon, I was shortly afterwards summoned by a booming voice shouting "Who made the tea?". I quickly admitted that it was me, and awaited thanks.

"There are no tea leaves!"

"No, Sir" (one always called the Manager 'Sir'; the staff were addressed as Mr. or Mrs./Miss) "I used the strainer".

"How can I read my fortune if there are no tea leaves?"

I quickly realised one had to do things to meet the requirements of others! This Manager was also a Bookies Runner; a man who took bets from people in the street and placed them with a Book Maker. This was before Betting Shops, and you had to have an account to bet off course. The 'Runner' was paid a small commission. Our Manager supplemented his income in any way he could! Indeed, customers often came into the Bank, went straight to the Manager's door, and having knocked, took their bets into the Manager. His desk did not have the usual Financial Times and Telegraph on display, but the Sporting Life, and Daily Express, open at the racing pages!

Betting by Bank staff was against the rules, but this Manager, if he saw something interesting in his tea leaves would 'instruct' his staff to place a small bet through him. It was many years later before I realised he was making commission for himself on every transaction. One day the leaves in his cup indicated the shape of a fish and there was a horse running at Kempton Park called 'Fish in Cup'. We all had to place 6d. on him, and it won. The winnings were reinvested on a horse in the next race, and we went through the card that afternoon. We lost it all on the dogs in the evening, but the Manager made a nice Commission that day!

He was a graphologist (reading people's handwriting), and wrote articles on fortune telling, etc., often selling them to American magazines who always paid quite well!

He suffered from gout, and came to work on a lady's bicycle, riding against the traffic down Ventnor, High Street, often wheeling with one foot on one pedal, and his stick on the other, with his swollen foot held at a right angle to the cycle.

I learned my first lesson in lending from this gentleman. Having at first refused to allow one young and not unattractive lady customer to cash a cheque, she asked to speak to him in his room. After a short while they both came out with large grins on their faces, the Manager holding his thumb up indicating the cheque could be cashed. Being young and innocent, (I am not so young now) I later enquired what had changed his mind. I was invited into his room, and after closing the door, he admitted that she had sat on the corner of his desk and pulled her skirt up above her knee. (This was well before mini-skirts!) All he said was, "…

how could I refuse her?" That was when I learned there was more to lending than in the instruction book....

Some years later, one man who often required some financial assistance (shall we say) asked for his usual £50 loan. I needed to know what he wanted it for, and his explanation was that he had to get some new false teeth. I commented that he had some in his mouth, and why did he need more? "Well, I had just finished dinner yesterday and, in going to the toilet, stood up and coughed just as I was about to pull the chain. My false teeth shot from my mouth straight down the pan!" He added that he had tried to catch them before they disappeared, but was too late. "But you have some in your mouth" I remarked. "Ah, these are my wife's, and I have to be home for her to eat her lunch". I lent him the money! I was usually rewarded by a nice piece of bread pudding or some green beans from his garden. Cash rewards were not allowed, but small gifts could be accepted.

When Credit Cards were introduced, we had to persuade as many customers as possible to have one, even if they did not use it. One such customer reluctantly agreed to have one. Three months later we were contacted by the Access office to say he had used the card and had gone over his limit; worse, he was not paying anything in to repay the debt. I was sent to his house.

He was delighted to see me as he wanted to thank me for the card. When it came it said he could use it to buy everything he needed, and he did so getting new furniture, carpets, crockery and wallpaper, etc. I was invited to sit on his purchases. "That is why I have come, you have not paid off anything for these items". "No," he said. "I did not want one of those cards, the one you sent me is perfect. The letter with it when it came said I could buy anything I needed, and I did, but it did not say anything about paying it back". He never did!

One rather eccentric couple would often come into the Bank and sometimes stay all day, trying to work out how much cash they needed to draw. One very hot summer's day he wore a full Arabian outfit including headgear, and said he had left his camel in the Camel Park at the back!

Whilst talking to him it was not unusual for him to fall asleep, occasionally waking up and usually saying "Yes, Yes" before returning to slumber; most reassuring! His wife was with him one day, and being somewhat embarrassed by his antics, she nudged him in the shoulder. When this did not work, she squeezed his thigh, when he opened his eyes, and exclaimed "Yes, please!".

At one time the Bank had small agency offices in the front room of a shop, or a house, which would open for just two hours a day, twice a week. At Wroxall, at 11.00am the local Publican would bring over a tray with tea and sandwiches, and the Policeman, Vicar, Postman and Shopkeepers would look in for refreshments and a chat! At Lake it was in the front room of the local Undertaker, and on more than one occasion a coffin (full) would have to be removed before we could open!

I was always happy to try and help eccentric customers. One such was a lady aged about 80 and of various mixed nationalities, and at first had some difficulty speaking English. This was right up my street, and as time went by, we became good friends. She was of some wealth and I was able to attract remunerative business for the Bank.

She used to seek my help with some words. She had a male friend who drove her car and was referred to as the chauffeur. The lady asked me what an 'ass' was, and knowing she liked animals I said it was a donkey (rather than another explanation for the word). She flew into a rage and said "…he is not going to call me a silly ass…". She came in one day wearing a feathery hat, and I complimented her on her appearance. She was pleased to say she went down to the beach the other day wearing this hat, and a sea gull nearly came and "shit" on her head. I suggested "sit" might be a better word, and she thanked me!

An Australian lady called one day to open an account – another job for me. I took her into the interview room when she said she had lost her husband. It was often the case that as it was not always possible to find a parking space, one person might come into the Bank whilst the other was parking the car. I said "… don't worry, he can come in when he is ready". "No" she said, "he's dead". I apologised for my error. She said "…it was his fault". Speaking in a broad Aussie accent she explained. "When we left

Australia he would take a plane which stopped at Singapore. I told him don't stop there, but he insisted. When we landed at Singapore, and walked down the gangway, he dropped down dead on the runway". "I am terribly sorry", I said. "No, don't be; it was his fault, but Quantas were wonderful; they sorted out the funeral, took me to the Crem, and got me on the next flight to England, but it did nearly spoil my holiday!" She added, "If you know of anyone going to Singapore, make sure you tell them to fly Quantas, because if their husband drops down dead they look after you wonderfully". I pass on the advice!

To end my talk, how about the NatWest Pig, dressed in blue trousers and a red and white tie I produced at the start. It is rarely remembered these days, but he was 'Maxwell', the spitting image of Robert Maxwell, who apparently turned out to be a bit of a pig himself!

CHAPTER 4
What The Papers Said!

(a) Before the Great War

Some years ago, the wife of a former printer with Lightbowns of Ryde, who used to publish the local Ryde paper 'The Isle of Wight Times', gave me several boxes full of copies of that paper covering periods between 1860 and 1930, which were saved by her husband from being dumped when the paper stopped publishing. These were from their archives, and gave a unique look back at the paper's past, and Island life in those years. With her consent I selected articles and advertisements from the papers and made a talk which many find fascinating. The following are just extracts from some of those papers, in random order.

Early papers rarely had photographs, so it was the skill of the journalist to 'paint' a picture of the event to provide the reader with an image of the time. One must also remember that many freelance journalists were paid by the number of words, or lines, they wrote!

Cost of Courtship 1903 –

To open the talk, I usually quote from a small article headed 'The Cost of Courtship'. It starts with a bill –

Mr. J.J. Smith Dr to Hesekiah Blodgers.

To 3 months use of parlour, Thursday and Sunday evenings	£3.	0.	0.
To gas and coal used for comfort, at 1/- a night which is very reasonable	£1.	6.	0.
To the old lady's trouble in keeping the children out of the parlour while you were with Maria		10.	6.
To broken rocking chair – which I paid for its being mended		3.	6.
To suppers at various times	£1.	7.	0.
To springs and upholstering damaged on Sofa where you and Maria used to sit together – say		15.	0.
Total	£7.	2.	0.

I want you to understand that if Maria, my daughter, has given you up, I haven't and won't do until you have paid for your pleasures. You can't come fooling around my house two nights a week without paying for the luxury. You've got to pay for your fun. If you don't I'll thrash the life out of you. You hear me? HB.

After reading this at one talk, a lady said she recalled that when she was courting her eventual husband around 1950, they were allowed to use the 'front room', although all that happened was that they sat there and talked! On the second visit there was a knock on the door, and when opened her father was standing there. He had come for the 'rent' of the room. Her boyfriend asked how much he owed, and it was agreed half a dozen eggs a night would be acceptable. So, thereafter he always turned up with six eggs!

In the 'Times' dated 7th May 1863, under Coach Accommodation, is noted - 'The coach (stage coach) from Blackgang to Ventnor commenced running on Monday, leaving Blackgang at 8.00 and 2.30, and returning from Ventnor at 10.30 and 6.00 pm. This is some three or four weeks earlier than usual, but from the very fine weather, and the increased number of visitors in Ventnor this spring, there is no doubt the proprietor will be fully repaid. One of the most delightful rides on the Island is from Ventnor to Blackgang, especially at this season of the year, when all nature is in its beauty, with the hawthorn in full blossom; there is scarcely a drive equal to it in any part of the kingdom.'

They discuss at length the need for the coach to start earlier in the year to meet the increased demands of visitors to Ventnor and the resultant demand for accommodation. They conclude '…This will soon be remedied when the railway is opened, and the pier finished for embarking and disembarking passengers from steamers.'

In the same paper, under Shanklin - 'Our Amateur Bands – Shanklin has felt the stimulus, given by the Volunteer movement, to the cultivation of instrumental music. There was a time when the strolling German bands had a monopoly of the supply, but, during the past eighteen months, two brass bands have been raised and efficiently maintained. Each band goes out once a week, and plays at the hotels and other places, which tends very much to enliven the village, and we think will be an additional attraction to visitors, whose constant complaint of a small watering place is that, notwithstanding its beauties and natural attractions, yet is so excessively dull.'

The 'Isle of Wight Times' of 25th June 1863 - 'Boat Race – West Cowes. It has long been the fashion to speak sneeringly of the manly prowess of tailers, but every day's experience tell us that – take them at their true values – they are not to be sneezed at. Monday being their holiday, two boats were manned from their respective establishments of Morgan and Gladwin, and as a good supper was to reward their efforts, it was imagined the struggle for superiority would be severe. The point of departure was from opposite the Docks to row to Medham Quay and back, at the starting the chances seemed even, but ere long the superior stamina and wind of Morgan's crew were so manifested that the losing crew threw down their oars in despair and resigned the contest.'

Several editions of the 'Isle of Wight Times' in 1863 included advertisements for 'cure-alls', usually with a letter of recommendation from a grateful purchaser of the product.

One, for Page Woodcock's Wind Pills, sold by Mr. Dixon, Chemist of Ryde, has a letter to Mr. Woodcock from a grateful husband – 'Dear Sir, I beg to add my testimony to the efficiency of page woodcock's wind pills. My wife had been afflicted for about twenty years with pain in the stomach and body, the violent belchings of wind were so dreadful that she might be heard all over the house, and indeed her life was almost a misery to her, the pain being so great and so frequent. She sometimes quite wishes for death to put an end to her sufferings. On three occasions after violent spasms in the stomach, she vomited a great deal of blood, at one time from three to four pints. She applied to various medical men, but to no purpose; so I resolved to get her to try your celebrated 'WIND PILLS'. After the first dose she obtained a comfortable night's rest, and gradually got better, and is now quite well. She has had no return of the bleeding, and does not suffer with wind, and eats two or three times as much as she did before.'

Holloway's Pills offered the 'best remedy in the world' for such as – Bad legs; Bad breasts; Bunions; Chilblains; Soft corns; Gout; Lumbago; Piles; Sore nipples; Sore throats; Tumours; and Yaws' – and many more!

The cost of the celebrations for the wedding of the Prince and Princess of Wales in Ryde has led to a shortfall, and every member of the Committee was expected to contribute 13/6d towards the overspend.

In April 1863 there was a vivid description of a major fire, and following is just a selection from this:-

'Brading – Destructive Fire. One of the most destructive fires that has taken place for many years occurred on Saturday night at Lower Morton Farm, the home of Mr. John Munns and his family. It is situated on the road to Sandown, and was one of the prettiest roadside farmhouses between Ryde and Shanklin. The house presented with its old fashioned appearance and thatched roof, a specimen of the farmhouse of the last century (1700s)…. This attractive and lovely spot is now a heap of ruins, completely gutted by the flames, with only the walls remaining and its gaunt-spectre like chimney standing in the midst. As is usual with old buildings, it was assumed the fire had originated from a beam in the chimney. On the 1st of the month the chimney took fire, and the necessary means to extinguish it were made by making an opening for the purpose of introducing water. It having been effectively put out, as it was supposed, the following day the plaster was made good again.

However, on Saturday evening last some dresses were found to be on fire in a closet near the chimney. Water was applied, but it was observed that the wall was so excessively hot that on the application of the water it hissed from its extreme heat. It was thought the fire had been put out, and one of the daughters said so to a neighbour, who corrected the mistake by observing that flames were running round the thatch. In order to clear the house from smoke the burning dresses had caused, the doors and windows were opened; this producing a strong current of air, when flames were seen issuing from all parts of the roof, and in a quarter of an hour the whole of the upper part was in a blaze. …the flames continued to rage and their progress was fearfully rapid, and the appearance of the fire was awfully grand. A double line of men was soon formed who handed buckets of water from the pond which was a considerable distance from the house, and they saved several stables, barns and outbuildings. Messengers were sent to Ryde for an engine which arrived about 11 o'clock; returning to Ryde at about 6 o'clock on Sunday morning.

The whole of the horses, stock and poultry was fortunately saved with the exception of one unhappy pig who fell victim to the flames. The deeds of the farm were saved and all the plate and money, and also two of Mr. Munn's grandchildren who were in the house were saved. The property was insured for £150.0.0.

In June 1863 - 'Late Refreshing Showers – The recent rains have done wonders in changing the face of nature, everything previously appearing quite dried up. The oats and barley in our neighbourhood were quite stunted owing to the want of moisture; but now even that discontented being 'the farmer' puts on a cheerful countenance and confesses that things look better!'

In July 1863 a friendly game of cricket was reported, between the Ordnance Club of Southampton who challenged the men of Northwood on the Cowes Recreation Ground. 'The play commenced at about 11 o'clock, and continued throughout the day until 6.30 p.m., including the play of knife and fork on the viands provided by Webber. The game was strongly and skillfully contested, the men of Southampton showing themselves first-rate fieldsmen, and though victory did not crown their efforts, it must be confessed that they are most formidable opponents. …The necessity of getting ready for home precluded the Ordnance men from playing the second innings; however, all retired satisfied, if not pleased. We will give the score next week!' (They did – Northwood 116, & 95; Southampton 65.)

More sport in July 1863 – 'Amateur Pedestrianism. On Monday evening at 10 o'clock, a foot race of 100 yards took place on the Esplanade at Ryde between two men. The men on coming to their places presented a strange contrast, the one being long and thin, the other being short and stout. 2 to 1, and in some cases 3 to 1, was offered on the long'un, but the chances being so much against his corpulent rival, there were but few who would take the odds. A capital start was effected, and the men got off in good style. For the first eighty yards a very even race took place, but then, 'a change came o'er the spirit of the dream' and away went the little man wishing his long friend a short farewell – "Good bye, Bill" – and dashed in about six yards ahead of his astonished opponent. The race occupied about twelve seconds.'

In a recent Athletics television commentary of a long distance Walking Race, Steve Cramm mentioned that "…road walking was once called Pedestrianism and was one of the earliest athletic events, originating as far back as the 1700's…". In those days wealthy citizens who travelled in their horse drawn coaches had a 'foot-man' who had to walk beside the coach in case a horse was spooked and so avoid an accident to the passengers. They had to walk; running was not allowed. If they broke into running they could lose their job. To encourage this special walking, races were held between the footmen. They became so competitive that there were often bookmakers taking bets on the results; just as mentioned at Ryde in 1863.

'Inmates for Parkhurst – Another batch of female convicts was landed at the Commercial wharf in Cowes and conveyed in omnibuses to Parkhurst. The number landed was 30, and they appeared by their manners to be rather of a superior kind to many of our recent importations from Millbank.'

In the 'Isle of Wight Observer' of 4th July 1891, there is an advertisement for 'Allan's Anti-Fat' with drawings of a portly lady, marked 'before' and a slim one marked 'after'. 'Purely vegetable, Perfectly harmless, will reduce from two to five pounds per week; acts on the food in the stomach preventing its conversion into Fat. Sold by Chemists.'

In January 1904 another advertisement included a letter from Mr. Hickens of Ventnor. "It is now some time since I began to suffer from severe pains across my back and loins, caused by my kidneys being out of order. My back was very weak, and when I stooped or bent down it was hard to get straight again. The secretions from the kidneys were thick and darkly coloured and very painful. I was under several doctors, but I got no better. Then I heard of 'Doan's Backache Kidney Pills' and got some. I felt very much better after just a few doses, and I kept on with them and the result is I have lost the pains in my back, my kidneys are acting freely, and the secretions are now quite clear!"

A report of a case before the County Bench. 'Alfred Wright was charged with having been drunk and disorderly on Christmas Day at 11 p.m. The policeman said he was walking up and down the road swearing and enticing another man to fight. He complained that another man had assaulted him and had a bruise on his hand. Witness found out afterwards that he had been fighting the lamp post.'

Some items are very sad, and in themselves may have had an effect on future action. In 1908 the report of the following Coroner's Court on a fatality appeared. It is headed 'The Shanklin Child Burning Fatality; The Danger of Flannelette'.

'The father of the unfortunate child told of what happened as he knew it. He said the child was six years of age on the Tuesday before the accident. He and his wife had had breakfast about 7 o'clock, after which he went down the garden to see his pigs, while his wife was preparing a piece of toast for each of the children. This she placed on the plate rack over the kitchener, leaving the door of the kitchener open to make the place warm and comfortable for the little ones when they came down to breakfast, which was soon after 8 o'clock. The mother had gone upstairs to bring the children down, and the little one, Alice Maud, ran on ahead of her mother and went and stood on the fender to reach her piece of toast. The father did not see the accident happen, but his wife had told him the circumstances, and he came rushing into the house on hearing screams. He found the little girl all ablaze, her flannelette nightgown being completely burnt away. "The fire ran like paraffin", he remarked. He took his coat and put it round the child and in a minute or two the flames had been put out. The little woollen vest he cut away; that was not burnt very much. The father put her to bed and she remained sensible all day long, and after an hour or so he said she was in no pain, but passed away on Friday morning in her sleep.

A verdict of accidental death was recorded but the Assistant Coroner asked that the accident be taken as a warning to people using flannelette in future.'

Many advertisements appear around the early years of the 20th century for what was called 'Coupon Insurance'. On production of a coupon from a newspaper or other publication, in the event of an accident, a sum of money could be claimed. The following appeared in the 'Isle of Wight Star' on 18th May 1912:-

'General Accident Fire and Life Assce. Corpn. Ltd. – Coupon Insurance Ticket.

£100 (one hundred pounds) will be paid to the next-of-kin of any person who is killed by an accident to the passenger train or tramcar in which the deceased was travelling as a ticket-bearing or paying passenger, or who shall have been fatally injured thereby, should death result within one calendar month after such accident. provided that the person so killed or injured had upon his or her person, this page, with his or her usual signature, written prior to the accident, in the space provided below, which together with the giving of notice within seven days to the above Corporation, is the essence of this contract. This insurance only applies to persons over 14 and under 65 years of age, and holds good for the current issue only. No person can recover under more that one Coupon Ticket in respect of the same risk.

Signature ....

This Coupon must not be cut out, but be left intact in the 'Island Star' as that being dated forms the only evidence of its currency.'

(Can you imagine a wife saying to her husband just starting off on a railway journey "Have you signed your Coupon in the 'Star', just in case you are killed", and even hastening his death from such an accident if he was still alive but failing after, say, 29 days from the accident!!!)

1913 'Well-Sinker's Terrible Death. A man was engaged in sinking a well and had reached a depth of 150 ft when it was found necessary to use blasting charges. One had been put in, but after waiting some time the shot did not explode, the Well-Sinker went down again to ascertain what was wrong. He had just reached the bottom when those at the top heard an explosion. The deceased, it is said, went down singing!'

1912 'Breach of Promise Damages. In the London Sheriff's Court, Miss Ethel Bellord was awarded damages of £100 against Laurence Firth of Rangoon for breach of promise of marriage. Firth made the acquaintance of Bellord when she was aged 12 and he was 22! When the lady was 18 the Defendant proposed marriage, and was accepted, Miss Bellord being received by the Defendant's family. In 1908 Firth went to Rangoon as Commander of a tug, and wrote home most passionate love letters, and altogether over one thousand were received. There was an interval between the letters from December 1910 and February 1912 during which time he had been living with a Burmese woman who had three children by him. This news affected Miss Bellord's health!' (The Rogue!!)

(b) During the Great War 1914–1919

Clear propaganda letters were included to make it look as if the soldiers were having quite a good time fighting for their King and Country; humorous articles about life in the army; to vividly horrific descriptions of the atrocities of War. Without either radio or television to relay the news, it was the papers who alone had to do so as best they could!

The Worcester Regiment was stationed on the Island, and a regular article around the 1916 period was of the antics of 'Ginger Mudds'.

Ginger Mudds is the despair of his Corporal; he is losing his hair and rapidly decreasing in weight. The other day Ginger met an officer in Ryde and instead of saluting, nodded genially. The officer objected and voiced his objections somewhat luridly. Ginger explained that he had rheumatism in his arm and shoulder and it hurt him to salute – and he didn't think it mattered because the officer was only a second-lieutenant. That evening he met the same officer again, and mindful of his wigging in the morning, Ginger stopped, faced the officer, clicked his heels together and saluted – with both hands. Of course there was more trouble and Ginger was 'for it' again. He confided to one of his room mates the next day that he was 'fed up with the bally army, the blighters were never satisfied!'

A few weeks later Ginger is in trouble again, rather serious trouble too. Poor innocent Ginger is philosophic, and his troubles usually sit very lightly upon him. But the trouble this time is rather serious, and Ginger is worried. You see, he didn't know the officer was a big-gun; he didn't know he was an officer at all. The poor fellow said he thought the said big-gun was a Salvation Army Officer because he had a red band round his hat. Ginger Mudds was appointed officer's orderly for the day and he went to report himself to the said officer – not the big-gun, only a comparatively small one, a rifle so to speak.

On entering the room Ginger omitted the salute and merely remarked in a friendly, confident way that he was the officer's orderly for the day. Ginger somehow omitted the 'Sir' also, although he ought to have known better. The officer wasn't a bad sort and said to Ginger "That is not the way to report yourself. You are only a youngster, I suppose, and don't know any better. Just sit down there in my place and I will show you how you should enter the room and report yourself". Ginger seated himself comfortably and unconcernedly in the officer's chair and awaited developments.

The officer left the room, entered again, halted three paces from Ginger, clicked his heels smartly together, brought his hand to the salute and said "I'm your orderly for the day, sir". Ginger smiled at him kindly for a moment, shifted himself into a more comfortable position, and replied "All right my man. You can shove off again, I shan't want you today". Poor Old Ginger!

1918. Mrs. Rayner of Ryde has received the following letter from the late Sergeant Rayner's platoon officer concerning that gallant young soldier's death.

'Dear Mrs. Rayner,

I expect you will have heard of the death of your son Sgt. Rayner of the 1/8th Hants. Regiment. He was hit while he was advancing over 'No Man's Land' to attack the Turkish trenches, and although he got back as far as the dressing room, and received every attention he died very shortly afterwards. He was not in great pain, but was able to have a cigarette and a drink of tea at the dressing station. I saw him just as he was wounded and although hit himself he kept on calling "Go to it, D Company!" He was a gallant soldier and a splendid NCO. All his men loved and respected him. Please accept my deepest sympathy in your great loss. You have every reason to be proud of having bred so gallant a son."

1917. Heroes all. In France, during bombing practices, a live bomb rolled back into the trench which was occupied by the thrower, an officer, and Sgt. Healy. All three ran for shelter, but Healy fearing the others would not reach the shelter in time, ran back and picked up the bomb which exploded, mortally wounding him. He had previously performed other acts of distinguished gallantry.

1918. Mrs. Price of Ryde received a letter from her son, Private Price RMLI who has been a prisoner of war in Germany since April 1917. He states that his health is excellent. On the day he wrote he received a private parcel in good condition, and two pieces of clothes from his headquarters at Gosport and a food parcel from the Prisoners of War Comforts Fund. The food parcels were arriving regularly and he was now fatter than when captured!

Late Sapper Ash – Mrs. Ash has received a letter from Colonel Mainprise RAMC stating that her husband had died of wounds. "You probably know this hospital was shelled by the enemy, and part of the block in which your husband was lying sick was knocked down and he received a very severe shell wound in the thigh, fracturing the bone. We are all especially sad at your husband's death because he built our mess tent a very fine fireplace, which has given us a great deal of comfort and pleasure this bitter weather. To think that the noble fellow who built it died on account of being in our hospital which he and his comrades mended up for us is too sad. On behalf of my officers and myself may I offer you my deepest sympathy. May God comfort and support you." (You can always find something good to say about anyone!)

Even as late as 1918 Military Tribunals were still being held for men up to ages over 40.

Lawrence Weeks (40), single, said he had an invalid mother whom he came home to support in 1901, and who was 68 and confined to her bed. He had also had an invalid sister who had died. The Chairman asked what he was doing of national importance? Weeks said he was working an allotment of 32 rod, part-working it with a man who had gone to sea. The Mayor commented "The tribunal think you are doing work of importance, and you will be excused other work. Get on with your garden!"

Maurice Riddett (39) single, said the difficulties were greater than when he was given exemption before. His book-keeper was within the new military age and would probably have to go; his office porter was also within the age; and his shorthand type writer would soon be of age. That would leave himself, one other man and a boy in knickerbockers. Temporary exemption 6 months.

Charles Davis, a hairdresser appealed as having a one-man business. He had been given exemption before but was now appealing on personal grounds. He was married with two children. He had lost one brother in the War and had two others serving. He did hair cutting and shaving at the County Hospital and Hazelwood, and put in night work at Hazelwood with the Red Cross. He was paid for work for private patients, but not for the wounded. Exemption 3 months.

Island War wedding 1918. A real war romance surrounds the wedding of Lucy Dart and Lt. Dawson, the poster artist. Miss Dart whose home is in the Isle of Wight had been singing a great deal for the wounded and at one of these concerts she met Lt. Dawson who was doing lightning sketches. When he saw this pretty girl with chestnut curls she seemed to him the living realisation of the 'Dawson Girl' he had been drawing for a long time. The wedding took place at Carisbrooke Church and was one of the prettiest and most romantic marriages of the season.

Match shortage. The match shortage is causing the adoption of a most drastic economy among smokers. Five cigarettes were lit in the High Street the other evening with one match, and the man who lit the match looked round to see if he could find another man who wanted a light, as he said it was a pity to 'waste' the match!

Grave & Gay – 1914. Wife; "I must say I think you are the worst dressed man in the town." Hubby: "And you, my dear, are the best dressed woman, which accounts for it!"

Small son, after his father had missed the golf ball for the sixth time, "What's the little white ball for, Papa?"

The man who answered an advertisement offering people a recipe to prevent beer going flat received the reply "Drink it!"

"Last night", said Mr. Henpeck, "I dreamt that I was in heaven". "And was I there with you" his wife asked. "Didn't I say it was heaven" he replied.

Letter to 'Isle of Wight Times' – 1917.

In consequence of the great number of inquiries which I have received from British subjects, may I, through your columns, point out that natural born British subjects are quite free to enter the Isle of Wight without permission or a passport.

Chief Constable I.W.

Brunswick Street. Your pithy little note in Town Talk last week should certainly be acted upon. There is surely no reason why we should continue to use a German name in our street nomenclature, and the sooner it is altered the better the majority of the citizens will be pleased. Your suggestion of 'Barton Road' is an excellent one, and I heartily commend it to the notice of the authorities. It would be a graceful acknowledgement of all the Mayor (Mr. Barton) has done for Ryde.

1918 – New Coupon Values. In a list of food which could be bought using meat coupons is – Horseflesh, with bone 1 lb 12 oz; cooked 1 lb 6 oz; without bone 1 lb 6 oz; cooked 1 lb.

And finally, others ways of getting support for the War effort!

From the Worcester Regiment (remember Ginger Mudds above?).

Special Women Patrols. Sir, please allow us through the medium of your paper to ask the persons concerned what authority they have to question young girls as to their ages, etc. and to flash upon them electric lights when walking out with soldiers. It is not only an insult to the girls, but to the men who, coming from respectable homes, have given up a great many pleasures, and to whom a few hours spent in the company of a lady friend is a luxury.

If these women are members of a religious body, as we are given to understand they are, we cannot imagine why they should judge others capable of crimes which they themselves would never dream of committing. Judge not – lest thou be judged. Can these women find nothing better to do? If not we would suggest they sit indoors, perhaps in the Parish Room, and knit socks for the boys in the trenches, but it may be they cannot sit still and know that other people are enjoying themselves.

From 'Not a Pen Driver'

(I usually ask the audience what they know as 'Flappers'. The reply is usually, young girls, 1920s, short skirts, short hair, the Charleston. In Ryde in 1918 they had a different role!)

In your last Thursday's paper you had something to say about the Flappers. I am a Flapper, I am happy to say, and although I cannot wear the King's Uniform to serve both my King and Country, I feel I am doing my bit in keeping the 'Khaki Boys' happy and jolly in my company. As to our short skirts and hair down our backs, this War makes us old before our time, and why should we Flappers wear long dresses and put our hair up just to please you? You are only jealous because we Flappers are true to our colour, and won't look at you, a Tailor's Dummy! There is still plenty of 'khaki' left to make a suit to fit you.

(Raising my voice -) Go and be measured at the nearest recruitment office and get a free suit for Whitsun. You would feel a big brave soldier. You would have plenty of Flappers then, Johnny! It is only old men and slackers who don't don 'khaki'. 'Khaki' is the order my boy now-a-day. You wait until all the soldier darlings, 'Mother's joy and treasures' and our Flappers 'Honey jars' come home – you slackers won't half cop it, and serve you darn well right. Afraid to carry a gun – in case it hurts you! All honour to our brave 'Khaki' boys and to the dear little Flapper in her short skirts and flying hair, SHE IS NO SLACKER!

(And that's how the War was won!!!)

(c) Between the World Wars.

Many 'small advertisements' became popular at this time:-

Lady having larger house than she requires in best part of Ryde would let, part furnished.

Moleskins wanted 200/- per 100. Any quantity taken.

Wardrobes. Best prices given for ladies and gentlemen's left off wearing apparel.

Strong girl for housework; sleep in!

Two ladies would go as pair for winter months; house work and light cooking.

Cook, good, plain wanted, and a House parlour-maid, tall and experienced needed.

Families washing; large or small; good drying ground.

Girl wanted at once; good references.

Mangle for sale 20/-.

Pig expected to die made 16 stone weight after having Karswood Pig Powders. 12/-.

Ladies, Blanchard's Pills are unrivalled for all irregularities, etc., they speedily afford relief and never fail to alleviate all suffering. Blanchard's are the best of all pills for women.

Young lady desires afternoon engagement in Ryde; care of child or invalid; do needlework; not particular!

House for sale, six rooms, usual offices, garage, stable. Vacant possession £650.

Good home wanted for child, 18 months, full particulars given. 10/- weekly; pram and clothing provided; permanency. (Not in advert – little blighter won't stop crying!!!)

Yarmouth IW – Pretty detached bungalow for sale; brick built, rough cast, tiled, 4 rooms, scullery, attic, store for oil coal etc., bath, company's water, indoor sanitation. 1½ acres land, fruit trees, sheds, poultry houses; fine view of downs, etc. £775.

Pram for sale, strong, comfortable, suit delicate child up to 10 years; reasonable.

Artificial Teeth (old) wanted   4/- per tooth.

1920   At a meeting of the Food Control Committee one member enquired how it was that butter could be had in Newport for 3/6d a lb whilst in Ryde it was 4/-. The Chairman supposed it was because the neighbouring town was nearer the farmers. The Clerk remarked that shopkeepers stated it was not the leisured but the working classes who bought butter. They have the money, the middle classes do not!

1922   Workhouse Dietary – Major Dennis raised a question at the meeting of the Board of Guardians as to whether butter could be substituted for margarine in the dietary, as it was plentiful and cheap. Mr. Minter exclaimed "What? Cheap?" Major Dennis said there was nothing in margarine and he thought they ought to give something better now. Mr. Minter: "There is margarine and margarine". No alteration was made, Mr. Dabell saying that some of the people preferred margarine.

1920   Marriage and parenthood. At a meeting of the British Women's Temperance Association, the County Medical Officer of Health said he thought there was a good deal of sense in the practice in China where they paid their doctors whilst they were well, but when they were sick they did not! He also said, to much applause, that he was in favour of a certificate of health being required in the cases of those about to marry.

1920   National Rat Week. A hue and cry after rats will begin today, the first day of the second 'national rat week'. Every man, woman and child is expected to kill and slay at least one food destroyer. The new Act comes into force compelling Local Authorities to exterminate rats and mice within their borders. The Rat Week in October last was productive of millions of casualties, but it is predicted that this total will be eclipsed after this new hunt if poison is well and truly laid, and if sticks are stout and in enthusiastic hands.

1920   Violet James (10½) was charged with the theft of a lady's umbrella, value 10/-. It was stated she had absconded from home and committed the theft from a friend's home. Her mother said she thought it was a mania, the child had to steal anything she saw, and she simply could not help it. They had beat her and tried everything to stop it but without effect. The Chairman said "It seems an extraordinary thing, I can't understand it. Have the pictures anything to do with it?" – She has been going to the picture shows since she was three or four years old! There were other offences. Ordered to be sent to the Industrial School at Poole until she was 16; the parents were ordered to pay 10/- a week for the child's maintenance.

1921   Australian Team's visit. The donkey at the wheel which draws water from a deep well at Carisbrooke Castle, entranced the Australian cricketers. They were entertained to lunch by Gen. Seely, the Lord Lieutenant of Hampshire, at Brooke House, and broke their charabang journey from Ryde to visit the Castle. One of the Australians took the place of the donkey and provided an 'old world' snapshot for the others!

1921 Flower Show. First annual show of the Wootton Horticultural Society will be held in Mr. Souter's field in Kite Hill, on 18th August. A novel feature is open to members of Wootton Women's Institute only, the exhibits will include leather gloves, basket work, rush work, and knitted and sewn garments. Is the excellent visit and lecture on the subject by Miss Preece responsible for this entry?

1923 Gaming at Ashey. A man from Bristol was sentenced to two months hard labour for unlawful gaming at Ashey Racecourse. Police-Sgt. Rogers said prisoner was running a Crown and Anchor board with a crowd, including confederates, around. On the approach of the police he made a rush but was arrested. On him was found another unlawful game known as 'Picking the Garter'. The Chairman asked, "Can we have a demonstration of this game, we don't understand it?" Supt. Salter said "The prisoner will give it". The Magistrates Clerk said "I am afraid this is a public place!" The prisoner had a bad record for similar offences and had been sentenced for bigamy.

1925   An extraordinary lamb. At New Farm recently, a lamb was born with two bodies, eight legs, one neck, a curious head with two eyes, two mouths, and four ears. (Clone that and you would solve the meat problem! It was often the case that freaks of nature such as this were stuffed and displayed in shop windows to attract attention from the public.)

1926   An item from 'Rural Walter's Diary'. Sunday, January 24th. Went for a little stroll, Wootton Common, Lynn Shute (lovely basket of Primroses), White Hart (Havenstreet, 12 noon). Felt overjoyed, and burst into poetry:
>   Sweet peaceful Village, Haven of Rest
>   Air soft and balmy, and Sprouts of the best!

1926   W.I. Meeting. Motto for the month. "What is the use of patience if you cannot find it when you want it!"

1926   The Island Federation of Women's Institutes will be interested in a book published by Mr. Robertson Scott giving an account of this great movement. The W.I. has been described as 'the most important body formed during the century'. Proof of its importance may be found in the fact that it has been subsidised by the State to the tune of no less than £50,000. In England, Wales and Scotland there are over four thousand branches with a membership of a quarter of a million, and yet it is only ten years old. The organisation is democratic, non-party, and non-sectarian, and membership costs only two shillings a year! Mr. Scott tells us here of the fine work it has done in the fostering of handicrafts, music, folk dancing, drama and agriculture. Not the least of its good works is the strengthening of intercourse and mutual help in the more sparsely populated parts of the country.

1929   Public Lavatories at Seaview. At a meeting of St. Helen's Council, it was proposed to spend £725 for provision of public lavatories in Seaview.
   It was proposed to have two stories, the bottom portion for men and the top for women. One councillor stated that if they put a

lavatory where no one could grumble the thing would be useless. Mr. Odgers said "Have you any idea of the amount of crime of a disgusting order perpetrated in public lavatories?".

1930   Old Age Pensioner Cautioned. An old age pensioner was summoned for disorderly conduct. PC Barber said he saw the defendant put his fingers up to his nose to a young lady. He spoke to him, and shortly afterwards he put his fingers to his nose at him, and made an insulting gesture. He had received numerous complaints of defendant's conduct. Defendant said he only did what had been done to him many a time this last year or two.

He was let off with a caution. "Will you promise not to behave like this again in the future?" Defendant, "I hope the police will stop other people doing the same to me".

1932   A Newport Star. Miss Marion Lincoln, a young Newport girl, who is now at home for a rest after two months' engagement in non-stop variety at the Windmill Theatre in London, received very favourable notices of her performances from the London critics.

1932   King's Bounty. Mrs. Brown of Totland who gave birth to triplets has received the King's Bounty of £3 last week.

1939   Has it ever occurred to you that you get one pennyworth of heat with one pennyworth of light, by using gas for lighting? Ryde Gaslight Co.

And then there was another War!

CHAPTER 5

H.M.S. Fidelity
& The Chale Commandos

Of all the talks which I give, this has proved to be the saddest and yet most enjoyed of them all. It tells of one of the most extraordinary events to take part in World War Two, and if it had succeeded might have changed the whole course of the war. It involved some of the most influential people, and yet even today the truth remains uncertain. In an extraordinary way, almost every time the talk is given, someone in the audience comes up with a story of their own which adds to the interest of the event, and at the same time confuses it even more!

I remember when I was a very young child, just after the end of the Second World War, my father would look up at the cliff in the area of Blackgang Chine and remark about seeing young soldiers, whom he called 'The Commandos', jumping off the cliff holding onto a long rope and reaching the beach below in three or four jumps (we call it abseiling today), and then climbing up the rope and doing it all over again, time after time, day after day. I always got the impression he never knew why, and neither did anyone else! And yet the young Commandos were living in homes in the village at Chale, taking part in village activities, and very quickly making deep friendships with local people, all within a short 4 months period in 1942.

For many years the reasons behind their activities were unknown, and the whole episode was regarded with great secrecy. Books were written, and it was believed an attempt to produce a film was considered, but there was so little factual evidence that little came of it. It was not until Peter Kingswell, who had lived in Whitwell, on the Isle of Wight, set about researching the story, and eventually produced the superb publication "Fidelity Will Haunt Me Till I Die" in 1980, that some evidence of what happened came to light. Extensive research, contacting many leading military and political figures from the wartime, posed an enormous task to produce the truth. He faced difficulties in getting the book published and eventually did so through the Royal Marines Historical Society; it was not until then that people who had actually lived in Chale during the period the Commandos were there were able to learn a little of what went on, and even then some could hardly believe it!

I had spoken with local residents and gained some knowledge of the period, but this was often confusing; I had myself been slightly involved too. I gained a small reputation of being a local historian, and I recall being approached by a visitor at Chale Show who asked if I knew where the Chale Spies lived. I assumed they were referring to the two French people who were involved with the Fidelity project (there were rumours of other foreign spies in Chale during the war, but they were not French!). Although I was able to give information from Peter Kingswell's book, clearly the questions indicated there was far greater interest in the subject and I also asked questions of local people, who lived in Chale during the war. Another book on the private lives of Claude Péri and Madeleine Bayard, by Edward Marriott, published in 2005 by

Picador, added to the extraordinary circumstances, and enabled me to produce a reasonably truthful and interesting talk.

My story relates to the lives of two, possibly three French Agents, a ship which became known as H.M.S. Fidelity, and the many lives their extraordinary actions had on the population of a small village on the Isle of Wight in the midst of war in 1942. An event which even the British Admiralty noted in records held at the Public Record Office as "...I have been led to believe that the only honest incident in the whole of FIDELITY's history is that she sank".

But I must start at the beginning; and there were several!

Firstly, in England in 1920 where a merchant vessel of some 2,450 tons was built and purchased by a French firm to carry goods around the Mediterranean and West African coastal ports, and named 'S.S. Le Rhin' (The Rhine). By 1939 and the outbreak of the Second World War she had led a mainly unadventurous life.

In the 1930s, two people who were to play a leading role in this story met in what was then French Indochina, now Vietnam. One, Claude Péri, born in Corsica in 1903, had had an adventurous life and received severe injuries. The other, the daughter of a French family from Paris, Madeleine Bayard. She too had led a hard life in her early adult years. They both became members of the French Intelligence Service and became Agents for the French Government.

Agents are not spies, as was once made clear to me; I had met two British Agents and soon realised I had made a serious mistake in calling them spies. As was explained, basically a spy works with a group to achieve set aims for their Government, an Agent works on his own to achieve a specific goal, a far more important role! (There are other differences, but that will do for this talk!)

Claude and Madeleine became close friends, I suppose we must say they fell in love, and for the rest of their lives would never be parted!

The lead up to the Second World War took Péri all over Europe, even into some of Hitler's innermost organisations. He grew ever more hateful of Hitler, and aimed to do all he could to end his power. As the war progressed, the Germans made headway across

Europe and into Péri's France, driving many of its citizens ahead of them. Péri was given the task of providing escape routes for French Agents to England, including a number of female Agents. He bought a merchant vessel in Marseille (the 'Le Rhin') and used her for the task. She was loaded with a mixed cargo which it is said he sold as and when he needed funds to run the ship. It is also said that he sold some and gave the proceeds to the British Government to purchase a Spitfire aircraft. I must say that different publications question whether he bought the ship, or hired her, but he never let her go!

With him when he purchased the vessel was his companion, Madeleine Bayard. He nicknamed her as a Mongrel Bitch - Claybard! – but they remained devoted to each other.

The 'Le Rhin' was fitted out with guns and on one trip sank a German vessel. Voyages were mainly to England, and the North African coast, but he would also occasionally stop off at Gibraltar, where he became acquainted with Admiral Sir James Somerville, (later to become Commander of the Far Eastern Fleet) who was to have a major influence on this story. Admiral Somerville gave the orders to sink the French Navy in Mers-El-Kebir to avoid it being captured by the German Navy, in July 1940.

By 1941, the number of fleeing Agents needing transportation to England, dried up, and he brought the 'Le Rhin' back to England and they were docked in Barry, in Wales, for refitting. Here the Royal Navy realised how important the ship was to the British war effort and so she was converted to a "Q" Ship; basically a disguise so that such ships could travel into enemy areas without recognition. The ship passed into the hands of Special Operations Executive (SOE), and as she was now a British naval ship she was given a new name – H.M.S. Fidelity. Claude Péri was now the owner and Commander of an H.M.S. ship, and as such he felt he should have an appropriate title and rank, and apparently without any official authority, gave himself the title Lieutenant Commander, and a uniform to match, and also a new 'English' name – Jacques (or Jack) Langlais (basically The Englishman). Madeleine Bayard adopted the name Barclay when she opened a bank account with Barclays Bank in Barry.

Madeleine rather liked the idea of being in the company of a British Naval Officer, and to have a suitable uniform. She, however, wanted more official recognition; after all she did not own an H.M.S. ship, so she proceeded to take up roles with the W.R.N.S. Her involvement brought her in touch with some of the highest personnel in the W.R.N.S. who were no doubt able to speed her 'promotion'. In a letter to Mr. Peter Kingswell when he was doing his research some years later, and in her own handwriting, Lady Cholmondeley (who was Chief Staff Officer to the Director of W.R.N.S. at the W.R.N.S. H.Q. in the Admiralty (H.M.S. Pembroke III) throughout the war) said "…I knew 'Barclay' well, and she was given the rank of Chief Officer (2½ stripes)".

Chief Officer Madeleine Barclay was trained as a Wren at the Royal Naval College Greenwich, which included training at Secret Intelligence Service (S.I.S.) in Section 'D' (the 'D' standing for Dirty Tricks). Here such as Kim Philby and Guy Burgess were on the staff, (and they became quite famous later!). Section 'D' and the S.I.S. are mentioned in several episodes of the excellent wartime series 'Foyles War', where Miss Pierce mentioned that they have foreign agents training with them! Remember Barclay was still a French Agent.

At the time of Dunkirk in 1940, when the majority of the British Army was evacuated and brought back to Britain, the Prime Minister Winston Churchill decided that the British Army would remain on British soil to defend our country until such time as we would be in a position to mount an attack on German occupied land. However, he realised that there would be a need to have specially trained personnel to make secret missions into occupied areas. He formed special groups to be known as 'Commandos', initially all made up of volunteers, mainly young men who were prepared to risk their lives for their country. They would be trained to do the specific task for which they were needed. They would have special training, and live with families rather than in billets, as part of the family, close to where they were training.

On 7th December 1941 Japan attacked the American base in Pearl Harbour, and brought Japan into the war. This had a major effect on British war plans, and Churchill, with Vice Admiral Louis Mountbatten, and Admiral Sir James Somerville (who had been in charge of the Mediterranean Fleet and who was to become Commander of the Far Eastern Fleet), and no doubt others, realised something drastic was needed to stop the Japanese. It would appear that this was something the new Commandos could be involved with, although the plans were somewhat extreme!

Somerville had met our friend Péri (he did not know he had taken the title Lt. Cmdr.) in Gibraltar and knew his ship was now part of S.O.E., as H.M.S. Fidelity. From this point the picture gets rather cloudy and we can only surmise what happened. Many of the published material contradicts itself; indeed, even from the Admiralty, as we will see!

I believe that probably Somerville suggested Jack Langlais, and H.M.S. Fidelity might be used to take a Company of Commandos to the Pacific to form an attacking force to, and hopefully land on, Japanese soil. The ship would need to be fitted out, and the Commandos would need to be trained. Southampton and Portsmouth would be ideal for the fitting, and there was the Isle of Wight close at hand for training. They already had a base on the Island at Upper Chine School, in Shanklin. Personally I think (although I have no evidence) that such a suggestion would have been of interest to Mountbatten (whose family through Queen Victoria came from the Isle of Wight) and Somerville (who had relatives who lived in Chale, and who are buried in Chale churchyard). Indeed, Somerville might well, as a boy, have stayed in that village, Chale, and might well have been to Blackgang Chine where the cliff terrain was similar to that found in places on the Japanese coast. This might be an ideal place to train a Company of Commandos for a landing in Japan. I have no better theory as to why, in the summer of 1942, military personnel began arriving in Chale on the Island.

In June 1942, Surgeon Lieutenant James Robertson was sent to Chale to arrange accommodation for the anticipated arrival of the Commandos and their Officers. A Scotsman, he had a wife and son who were to come with him, so his needs were different from some. He was to be the Medical Officer. At first he was offered accommodation at the 'Clarendon Hotel' (now the Wight Mouse Inn) but felt that it was inappropriate for a wife and child of 3 years, and took up accommodation with Mr. and Mrs. Morris at Cliff Terrace.

The next to arrive was Captain Wright, the Commander of 40 Royal Marines Commando "T" Company, who arranged for the medical base to be established in a large garage at the house 'Lowcliffe' at the inland end of Cliff Terrace. A very large map of the Isle of Wight is still fixed to the garage walls there. Tents for a base and daytime accommodation were set up next to 'Lowcliffe', which itself was Capt. Wright's base. With Robertson's help accommodation was arranged with local families in their homes for the Commandos, usually two in each home. There were many families in the village where the adult male members had joined the Services, and there was spare accommodation. These families were paid for accommodating the Commandos and the men also provided useful help in the homes.

Captain Wright commented that he found the village of Chale to be 'quaint', the residents 'reserved', and that they had a mistrust of 'overners' – little has changed!!

One house where the soldiers were living was 'Sealands', a large Victorian house near the edge of the cliff and in the grounds of Blackgang Chine. Here a Bofors anti-aircraft gun was set up, overlooking the English Channel. When fired it made a very loud sound. The lady who lived there, Mrs. Molly Barlow, told me that she kept rabbits in the garden, as pets, and for meat. When they arrived there, the Commandos let all the rabbits out, and she recalled seeing them trying to catch them with rugger tackles! In a letter she wrote "I can see them now, rolling about catching rabbits".

Mrs. Barlow continued "…Walter, a Commando (who lived at Sealands) used to sit of an evening composing concerts; he couldn't play any instrument; he just composed. Whether they were any good or not I never knew. They (the Commandos) all had unlimited firearms and ammo – we used to have great fun with targets made from cornflake packets put up on the fence round Sealands' lawn. One day, Walter winged Miss Aubrey's (an elderly spinster lady who also lived in Cliff Terrace) hat, with a .22 as she walked back home."

It was not long before our two principal characters in this extraordinary tale arrived on the Island looking for accommodation; Jack Langlais and Madeleine Barclay. One of the first people they met on arrival at Cowes was Uffa Fox, the well known boat designer, yachtsman, and eccentric who by the early 1940s had established a reputation with women. In a way there were similarities between him and Langlais. Uffa offered the two French Agents accommodation at his property at Puckaster, in Niton, but Jack Langlais, learning of Uffa's reputation with women, feared Madeleine might be attracted, declined. Even many years after his death, Uffa's reputation still exists, and I have found that I only have to mention his name in a talk, and women over a certain age react with a saucy grin! At a talk in late 2012, a clock fell off the wall in a Methodist Church Hall in Newport at the mere mention of his name! Uffa had spread the rumour that he could not sire children (which was untrue).

An Arthur Wheeler, a member of the Chale Wheelers, had a cottage which he had left empty when he moved to Cowes and which could be lived in by a family needing accommodation due to the war. Half way down the cliff at the end of Cliff Terrace, it was in an ideally secluded position, but also close to where the Commandos were training, and the cliff face they had to train on. This Langlais purchased in Madeleine's name, using her adopted surname of Barclay, so that, if anything should happen to him, she would have a home. They moved into the cottage. (A year or so later, after they had left, Uffa Fox also had a cottage close by!)

Known to many as 'Mad Jack' due to his life style, Langlais became a familiar sight in Chale; often frequenting the Clarendon Hotel and other pubs; making a close friendship with the C. of E. Rector, Rev. Constantine Sinclair, who was a fluent French speaker. Langlais was responsible for the general training of the Commandos in preparation for their secret mission in the Far East, although at this time, few other than Langlais knew what this was.

Barclay's role was that of gunnery training, and she was responsible for the Commandos' training, using live ammunition, often firing just behind their feet or over their heads if she thought they were not moving fast enough. On one occasion several of the soldiers took an old and unseaworthy fishing boat which had lain unprotected for some years and was leaking badly, and attempted to sail it from the shore. Not responding to Barclay's call to return to shore, she fired live ammunition just over their heads – they immediately returned!

There is a well recorded incident when one of the Commandos used the clock on the tower of Chale church as a target. Having seen the dials from the clock at close quarters when I took them to be repainted some years ago, there was no evidence of gunfire, but the Cock weathervane which used to adorn the top of the church tower does have marks. I feel the story should refer to firing at the 'Cock' and not 'Clock'.

After a short period, a Royal Marines Officer from the mainland came to inspect the training in Chale, and Langlais proudly took him to Sealands and showed him his Bofors gun, and proceeded to fire a number of rounds. He had not given notice of this, and on hearing the sound of the gun all along the South Coast from Bournemouth to Portsmouth, the Red Alert was sounded and it was assumed that the Germans had landed and the invasion had started!

Langlais was summoned to the Admiralty in London for a disciplinary hearing (one of many to be issued against him), but as an Agent, acting in the course of his duty, all charges were dropped. These visits are referred to in Lady Cholmondeley's letter mentioned previously "…he (Péri, aka Langlais) was a good friend and was often in my office after a Board of Enquiry had been ordered by some irate Admiral!"

On another occasion, he was summoned after someone had thrown a small plastic 'bomb' at a Southern Vectis bus which was holding him up.

Madeleine Barclay had many attributes. I am led to believe that she liked to sunbathe in the nude on the lawn outside her cottage which was thought to be totally obscured from view.

However, some young teenage boys found a vantage point on the cliff edge where a suitable view was possible (this a long time before Page 3) which added to their education! She did not take to the task of housework or cooking. On the Fidelity they had a black Frenchman known as Henri Deladier (or Edward Brown) who acted as their cook; he had joined them in Marseille, and may well have been another French Agent. He was summoned to come to Chale, and on one very hot day, arrived riding a bicycle. Approaching a group of boys outside the local school, he asked them in broken English where the soldiers were? (They were about 200 yards round the next corner.) The local policeman, P.C. Sampson, had not long before warned everyone at the school to be aware of strangers and that it was 'dangerous to talk'. Here was a man of foreign extraction asking about soldiers, so they directed Henri down the Military Road to Freshwater. He returned several hours later, most annoyed!

Barclay had set up a Youth Club with some of the younger Commandos and the older youth of Chale, in an attempt to bring her men into village life. Some Commandos made friends with local girls, and at least one became engaged. Every attempt was made to make them feel part of the Chale community.

Training increased, and specialised equipment, including landing craft, and motor torpedo boats were made available in Southampton. On one occasion, a landing craft was sailed round from Southampton to make a landing on the shore below Langlais' home. It was foul weather, and one of them broke an ankle. His comrades carried him up the cliff and knocked on the door of the house near to where Langlais and Barclay lived and asked for help. Edith Cole provided them with tea and helped them dry off their clothes before completing their journey to base. A few days later some cans, without labels, arrived at Mrs. Cole's house, and assuming they were tinned fruit, the family sat down the next Sunday to enjoy their reward; but they only had tinned peas for their sweet!

Langlais was provided with an American Jeep, the first to be seen on the Isle of Wight, which he used as a staff car. Regular visits were made by Langlais and Robertson to Southampton, and also to London, to plan the trip to the Far East. Motor torpedo boats, and Sikorsky seaplanes, were made available to take on board H.M.S. Fidelity.

At a talk I gave to the Shanklin Historical Society in 2011, at the end, a member of the audience asked if he could comment. He was not a member of the Society, but having seen a poster about H.M.S. Fidelity wanted to know if it was the same boat his father had worked, and sailed, on. It was, but he worked in Portsmouth Dockyard, and it was there he had encountered Fidelity. There is no mention in the books published about works in Portsmouth. This must have been to fit guns, etc. The man said his father spoke of Langlais, coming on board with 'his wife' in a Naval uniform (unheard of in those days), and that he had a pistol which he would fire at people on board the ship if he disagreed with their comments! He also mentioned a Belgian Agent who accompanied them on their visits to the ship – a Major-General Albert Guérisse, known as Pat O'Leary who organised the Pat Lines for escaping nationals in the war. Major-General Guérisse had been an associate of Péri in Marseilles and was clearly still involved with him. The gentleman's father had sailed on Fidelity, presumably on trials, but he had said it was a rusty unseaworthy vessel!

Eventually, in October 1942, almost as unexpectedly as they had arrived, all the Commandos who were living in Chale, left for further training in Scotland, still not knowing what their destination was to be, but telling their friends in Chale that they would probably never see them again! H.M.S. Fidelity sailed from Southampton to Liverpool. On 17th December 1942 she was ready to depart. First Officer Madeleine Barclay was also aboard. Langlais was told this was not possible, but he replied – "No Barclay Aboard, No Ship". He refused to sail without her. They both sailed on Fidelity to join a convoy in the Atlantic on their way to the Far East. She sailed with a collection of French engineers as crew who had been with her since the Mediterranean days; over 32 R.N. personnel; 53 R.M. Commandos; and other Officers including James Robertson, Madeleine Barclay, and Lt. Cmdr. Jacques Langlais in command.

The weather became atrocious; and they were attacked by

German U Boats. The convoy's Commanding Officer's ship was sunk and Fidelity took on board as many survivors as it could take. One of the Sikorsky planes crashed beside Fidelity, and with depth charges on board, exploded as it sank, dislodging Fidelity's engines, slowing her down. By now she had over 400 men on board. One of the motor torpedo boats went off on a reconnaissance trip, and on returning on 31st December 1942 they could only find wreckage where Fidelity was supposed to be. Their 6 crew were the only known survivors; there is no record of anyone from H.M.S. Fidelity being picked up by other vessels.

When the news of the loss reached Chale there was great sadness, and this is reflected to this day. A special Memorial Plaque is placed in Chale church, and a wreath is laid every Remembrance Day in memory of those who were lost.

Mary Robertson, wife of Lt. Surgeon James Robertson, a trained nurse, and who had undertaken duties as the District Nurse before his departure, was now a widow with a son, Campbell. They returned to Scotland, her home. However, a few months later they returned to Chale and Mary Robertson took up the duties of the official District Nurse until around 1947. Mrs. Robertson became quite friendly with my mother, and Campbell used to stay with us while she was making her rounds.

- -

Books were published; accounts of the events of H.M.S. Fidelity made; and stories written. Often they contradicted themselves.

Relatively recently I was lent some extracts of official Admiralty documents which are available at the Public Record Office at Kew under ref. ADM 199/1320. From short extracts I have again taken small parts which I feel demonstrate just how complex the story was, and that it is certain the full truth will never be known!

Extracts from Ministry of Defence, Naval Staff Duties (Historical Section) sent 30th July 1990:-

"…I have heard the suggestion that the Fidelity was bound for some 'secret mission' more than once, and decided to research further… It is unfortunate that the paperwork surrounding

Fidelity's loss can only be described as a nightmare of official inertia, leading to rumour and speculation – which persists to this day. You need to read the documentation in full to get the complete picture."

From Director of Plans, Admiralty, 15th May 1943 (the ship sank on 31st December 1942):-

"...in view of the secret nature of the operations on which Fidelity was employed it was desired that as little comment as possible should be aroused in the Press on the loss of this ship, the matter was discussed verbally to decide how the Commanding Officer should be described. It was agreed the ship should be described as an Auxiliary vessel, and the Commanding Officer as a Free Frenchman. The D. of P.'s representative pointed out that Commander Langlais had no use for any kind of Frenchman, either Free or Vichy, and in fact would as soon fight them as the Axis.

The D. of P.'s representative did not see the actual wording of the communiqué before it was issued. He is sure of this because his first reaction on seeing it in the Press was to ask for police protection in case Cmdr. Langlais should be a survivor and should see the communiqué as issued. (No body was found.)"

From Admiralty notes, dated 15th September 1943:-

"The whole career of the Fidelity has been 'phoney'. I know nothing of it, deliberately, so that I shall not speak out of turn when heckled. The question of motorboats, seaplanes, etc. from whom there were survivors makes the whole situation more complex. It does, however, seem clear that the matter has been clumsily handled from the Admiralty end."

"I have been led to believe that the only honest incident in the whole of Fidelity's history is that she was sunk."

"...if there had been any 'phoney' business the Admiralty would have had enough sense to invent a plausible lie and tell everyone the same story."

From AD of Air, dated 22nd September 1943:-

"...I agree with you that the position has been handled in a most unfortunate way."

"The Directorate of Naval Intelligence concern was with the ship's company. Her real sponsor was Admiral Somerville, who knew the Captain, Cmdr. Langlais at Gibraltar. There was no continuity of supervision over her extremely unconventional Captain. There was an unfortunately worded Admiralty communiqué which gave the impression he was an Officer of the Fighting French Forces which was subsequently corrected in a private letter to the Sunday Times and not corrected by the Admiralty..."

"...In summary, H.M.S. Fidelity was bound for the Eastern Fleet but was torpedoed and sunk en route by U435. Her crew was French; her intended role, however, remains in doubt, and in view of this it cannot be stated with certainty whether the British servicemen were merely on passage or part of some other undefined mission."

And of Madeleine Barclay, she is believed to have been the only WREN to sail as an Officer in a fighting British Naval ship in the Second World War. An article in the I.W. Chronicle (Sandown Newspaper) in the 1950s described her as a "Buccaneer in Black Bloomers".

But I feel Lady Cholmondeley should have the last word.

"Yes, of course I had a great deal to do with all the Fidelity people. 'Barclay' was given the rank of Chief Officer (2½ stripes) in the WRNS and I knew her well, and of course Péri was a good friend, and was often in my office after a Board of Enquiry had been ordered by some irate Admiral! They gave me a fine Silver Salver with all their signatures inscribed on it…. The loss of the ship was a great blow to me – I had brought Péri together with Admiral Sir James Somerville who commanded the Eastern Fleet and they were on their way to join his fleet…."

CHAPTER 6

A Humorous Look at Church Burial Records, and a Look Round the Churchyard

I am delighted when I am told that this talk has proved to be the most enjoyable of them all. I had anticipated that some people in my audience may be put off by the subject; and indeed they may well be at first, but it is the overall interest which the local churchyard can convey to the unprepared!, and what you can learn from these records about how people lived in the past.

We are looking at two talks which I occasionally give, one the look at the Burial Records themselves, and the other a look around the churchyard, and inside the church itself. Both hold many fascinating secrets. My own research is all of Chale church but the general principles should be the same, certainly for Church of England churches.

Researching family history has become a common pastime, and can now be classified as an obsession for some. The availability of records on the internet has made research far easier, but I believe has taken much of the fun out of the game. But there is nothing better than getting your hands (or should I say, eyes) on the original records, and the most obvious is the headstone or memorial erected in a churchyard recording the life of the deceased person.

I recall a cousin of mine whose family originated in Chale and who went to Australia in the 1850s, contacted me to see if I knew where her ancestors were buried. When I showed her the headstones with her relatives' names on them, she sank to her knees and threw her arms round the stones, and hugged them. (Thank God she did not do that to me, although thinking about it, it might not have been such a bad experience.) As she put it, "I have now found my origins!"

But had she? There is a common feeling that a headstone marks the exact spot where a body is buried, but this is not always so. They are often erected some years later, and the exact spot may have been forgotten. In Chale several headstones are known to have been moved to allow for easier access along paths, etc. In some cases memorials have been erected when the body was not buried there; indeed there is a growing practice to bury cremated ashes of the same person in different churchyards.

Chale is a peculiar place, and often the people who lived there would do things 'differently'! May I explain some of the basics of a funeral and burial in a church and churchyard.

Traditionally bodies have been buried on an east/west line as evidenced by the findings on such as Time Team on the T.V. The head of the deceased is buried to the west, and the feet to the east. They are carried into the church in that way and placed in front of the altar for the service. They are then usually turned and carried out feet first. Then, at the graveside, they are buried as stated. That is unless the deceased is an ordained priest, when everything is reversed. They are carried into and out of the church head first, and buried with their head to the east and their feet to the west. Why? So that they will be facing their congregation on

Resurrection Day! (Watch what happens when you next attend a funeral and see if they do it right!)

So what happens if an error is made? Well, the law states that you cannot exhume (dig up) a body or even ashes, once buried. That is that you cannot bring the remains above the ground level, without special authority. What that also means is that, provided you do not bring the remains above ground level, you can turn them round and leave them buried.

In a copy of the I.W. Family History Society's Journal, it notes that in 1856 a boy had to climb a tree by his uncle's freshly dug grave in Northwood Cemetery to shine a lantern for his relatives to dig a circular hole – so that the coffin could be turned through 180° after it had been interred the wrong way round!

By the true meaning of the word 'headstone', the memorial placed on a grave being the name of the deceased, is placed at the 'head' end of the grave; i.e. the western end for ordinary mortals, but the eastern end for priests, and the inscriptions face east in most cases. So why is it that in each case where a priest is buried in Chale Churchyard, the headstone is at the western end of the grave?

Going further, another common feature of old graveyards is that the levels of the grass are often one or two feet higher than the surrounding road or path levels. Well, having dug the grave, and buried the coffin, there will always be a quantity of 'spoil' or spare earth left over which was just spread around on top of the surrounding land. Over the years, and numerous graves, the ground level rose. Now, if you come into Chale Churchyard from the Military Road side (south), and look both to the right (east) and left (west), the ground levels are much higher than the road and paths. So that's OK. Now look at the headstones on the right hand side, and other memorials (there are several 'box' memorials in the area). The inscriptions all face west when they should face east! Does this mean that everyone buried in this area is buried the wrong way round?

But then look again. Whilst all the headstones face west, some, in the centre of the area, are only some 12" or 18" apart. There is no way a coffin could have been buried in that space unless they are buried upright! In which case, you could say it does not matter which side of the headstone the inscription is written. Now that is Chale for you!

Pass on round along the path leading to the small gate in the eastern wall by Church Place. All the headstones are on the right side, and there are quite a lot, and follow the line of the path, which is by no means straight, and the inscriptions face west! They must all have been moved at some time to make way for the path. On the left side coming into the main gateway, and on the left, along the small path, all the headstones face east, as they should. Or should they; have a closer look, all of the graves along by the eastern end wall of the church are either of priests or their families, and the headstones of all face east, but the priests should face west (but then you would not be able to see them well!). Now that is Chale for you!

Whilst we are still in the churchyard, we can see the Parish War Memorial; a very traditional design which was produced for local communities to erect and display the names of their own fallen in the Great War. Names for WW2 have been added. This memorial was bought by donations from the people of Chale and erected by the young men from the village, some of whom had fought in France, and survived. A sum of money left over was used to provide a hymn number board which hangs beside the pulpit in the church. And that is Chale for you!

There are several more War Memorials inside the church; one erected in 1917 (presumably the local benefactor who donated the memorial was convinced the War was all but over in 1917); others refer to the 1914/18 War, and the 1914/19 War. Two memorials list those who served, and survived, as well as the fallen.

In the north/east corner of the churchyard will be found what is just a very large stone – with a small plaque commemorating the 2nd Millennium, the Chale Millennium stone. Along the northern boundary of the churchyard are the graves of mariners who lost their lives in shipwrecks in Chale Bay, in particular that for the 'Clarendon'; but a lot more.

Nearby is a fenced tomb grave of Lady Elizabeth Cole, a daughter of the Earl of Derby.

To the centre of the churchyard and to the north of the church can be seen what is probably the most imposing memorial there, a figure of an angel in marble, and other imposing memorials in the form of a crown on a cushion, etc., all within a metal fence. This records the Reade/Hamilton family who were responsible for the formation of the Blackgang Mission (later often referred to as the 'Tin Church' in Blythe Shute – now a holiday home). They had moved from India where Mr. Reade had been a member of the Indian Civil Service in Madras, for health reasons. They were Baptists and on the first Sunday after moving to St. Catherine's in Blackgang, Mrs. Reade and her sister, Frances Hamilton, walked to the Baptish Church in Niton. On the way back they were horrified to see men drinking on a Sunday, outside the Blackgang Tap Inn. They returned shortly after and preached to them about the sins of drinking on a Sunday. At first their words were rejected and they were met with laughter. However, undaunted they returned the next Sunday and preached again, which became a regular occurrence. Soon a meeting place was provided in Blackgang Chine and this non-denominational body, based on the Baptist faith, was established as the Blackgang Mission. Its popularity lead to the 'Tin Church' being built where a full baptism bath was provided. They are all buried together and the imposing angel memorial was erected in their memory.

There were many stories of a ghost in Chale Churchyard, and it was said you could see it flying along on a dark night. What was happening was that the headlights from vehicles travelling along the Military Road from Atherfield shone on the 'angel' throwing an image of a winged ghost onto the houses in Church Place which actually moved along, and even back, when the cars turned direction!

Near this memorial is the grave of Christopher Smith, one of the founders of the Young Men's Christian Association (Y.M.C.A.), a very shy man who moved from London to live with the Reade family at Blackgang.

Also in this area is a small Yew tree, planted to mark the Millennium in 2000, raised from seed from the Yew which supposedly grew from the staff of Joseph of Arimathea. Saplings were distributed to churches throughout England, and the one in

Chale Churchyard is now flourishing at a great pace!

The western area of the churchyard was part of the Hearn bequest and houses graves from c.1935. Here will be found an enclosed area where the First President of the Hungarian Republic, Michael Karolyi, and his son Adam were once buried. Their remains were exhumed and taken to Budapest in 1965 where they were given a State Funeral. Once housing the churchyard waste dump, it was cleaned out and in 2009 Judith Karolyi, Michael's daughter and Adam's sister, came to Chale and unveiled a memorial seat to her father and brother in a delightful ceremony, Chale's own "State" occasion. The enclosure and the seat marks the burial site of two distinguished members of the Catholic faith who were buried in a C. of E. cemetery, because that was where they had expressed a wish to be buried. The seat provides a quiet resting place for the many visitors to Chale Churchyard.

But there is one grave which in some way has been a mystery, certainly in more recent times. It is a coffin shaped memorial surrounded by a metal fence, located just to the left of the entrance porch to the church. I have often been asked who was the Henry Johnson whose name it bears, being in such a prominent place beside the church itself?

Inside the church is a magnificent pulpit with a carving of Jesus and his disciples, bearing a small plaque which needs to be viewed on hands and knees. It records that the carving was the work of Millicent Johnson and given by her family to Chale church in 1861. What is the connection (if any) between the carver of this pulpit and the grave outside the porch? I used to dismiss it as 'a relative'.

A former cousin of mine, the late Mabel Nicholson, often said that she had a letter written by the lady who carved the pulpit, written to children at Chale School in 1863. This is now in my possession, but I have only recently read it in its entirety. I make no excuse in copying it in full here, because it gives a fascinating insight into the life of different classes of people in the 1860s:-

Sent to Miss Baker, Headteacher at Chale School, I. of Wight, Ingliterra, and sent to five pupils who she had obviously met on visits to the School: Alice Sprake, Eleanor Tross, Catherine Brown, Fanny Draper and Annie Wight.

Florence – January 13th 1863

My dear little Girls

   *It was a very great pleasure to receive your letter and
to hear so much interesting news about Chale. You must
have been very grateful to have been able to help the poor
Lancashire people (see below) to so precious a packet; it was
very kind of Mrs. Barton to give such a quantity of flannel.
You must have enjoyed making up such nice warm petticoats.
One of my brothers in India wrote me word that the men in
his regiment all Indians, subscribed of their own accord £50 to
send to Lancashire which was very kind of the poor black men
I think. At the same time I am glad that the poor Whitechapel
children were not quite forgotten this Christmas.*

   *We have had as cold a Christmas as you, you would be
sorry for the poor little Italian children, they have no comforts
such as a nice warm schoolroom and no comfortable fire in
their homes, but they all carry in their hands wherever they go,
even to church, little earthenware pots full of charcoal, but I
am afraid they do not get much warmth from them, there are
no fireplaces in their houses so when there is a severe Winter
the poor people suffer very much.*

   *Before we came here we were at Genoa; do any of
you recollect what great man was from there? Yes, it was
Christopher Columbus and the people of Genoa would have
nothing to say to him when alive. They have now made an
enormous marble statue of him in a square. The town is full of
beautiful palaces built of white marble and the churches have
the ceilings entirely of paintings and gold. The women wear
nothing on their heads but a piece of white muslin crossed in
front and very cold they looked. You would laugh could you
see all the houses in that part of Italy. They paint them all as
smart as possible, one with a window and a cat looking out,
another with a dog, sometimes a man with a cocked hat and a
young lady dressed very smart. It was quite amusing to drive
through a village, and besides the figures the houses are all
painted all over scarlet or yellow or green. All the Italians like
bright colours, on a wet day they all come out with umbrellas*

of every colour; even the plough boys in the fields carry them whilst following the horses, some blue with yellow spots all over, scarlet with green borders, and so on.

When we left Switzerland we had to cross the Alps to get into Italy, a long day's journey, we had six horses to drag us (in sleighs), and we went up and up for 7 hours before we reached the top. At first there were houses, and churches, and trees, but as we got higher they all vanished and there was not even a blade of grass, then we got into snow which fell thick all round us, and very desolate it was, the poor horses could hardly drag the heavy load and slipped down every five minutes. At different parts of the road there are little huts built which are called houses of refuge and are of great use to poor travellers who have lost their way in the snow or are benighted (lost in the dark of the night) and sometimes the road is blocked up by the fall of avalanches which is occasioned by the snow on the mountains which overhang the roads becoming loosened and falling. Sometimes a whole village has been crushed by an avalanche. So you may suppose that travellers are afraid of them and are glad to take refuge in one of these houses. After we had reached the top the descent was very rapid, and we soon left the snow behind us. The mountain we crossed is the Simpton (?) – Napoleon Bonaparte made the road over it when he wanted to take his army into Italy to conquer it.

You would like to see the orange and lemon trees covered with such quantities of ripe fruit, they look so pretty among the dark green leaves, but you are very fortunate children to be English, these poor little Italians are very ignorant and have not much care taken of them, very few of them learn to read or write.

By this time I conclude you have returned to daily school. I hope you all have had a pleasant Christmas and that this year will be a very happy one to you and all. Eleanor Tross and Fanny Draper will I trust be wise girls and try to improve themselves at home and not forget all they have learned now they are giving up school. Alice, will you remember me kindly to Martha Brown (the Infants school teacher), and say I hope

Ellen is going on well in her situation. I hope that Martha and all her little flock are well. I am glad to hear a better account of little Sarah Stephens. Lady Johnson (the writer's mother) sends her thanks for your messages.

And now my dear Alice, Eleanor, Catherine, Fanny and Annie, I must finish my letter. Give my kind remembrances to all who ask after us, and with love to yourselves, believe me, always your

Affectionate friend,

Louisa Johnson.

(Not the person who carved the pulpit – Millicent Johnson – but her sister.)

I find this letter is almost a geography, history, and social history lesson in one. How lucky indeed were those Chale children of 1863, and how clearly it paints a picture of life 150 years ago, written by a member of the aristocracy who was able to travel the world and tell of their experiences in such a clear fashion.

Firstly some explanations from the text. The Poor Lancashire People – due to over production of cotton in 1859 and 1860 which lead to a cut back in work in the Lancashire Cotton Mills, many factories closed and thousands were left without employment, and from being the most prosperous workers in Britain they became the most impoverished. From 1861 to 1865 a Cotton Famine or Cotton Panic struck Lancashire, and a Worldwide Appeal for help was made. From small village schools to the British Army abroad, indeed all over the world, help was sought. Chale played its part by making petticoats!

So who was the Henry Johnson buried near the church doorway. Sir Henry Allen Johnson, Bart., 2nd Baronet of Bath, son of Sir Henry Johnson, the 1st Baronet who was a Knight of the Bath and also a Knight granted by the King of the Netherlands. Our Sir Henry was also aide-de-camp to the Prince of Orange, and fought with honour in battles of the time. He had several children including Millicent (who carved the pulpit in Chale Church) and Louisa who wrote the letter above. It would appear the family originated in Ireland, but why and where were they living or staying in Chale in the 1860s and why was the pulpit carved so expertly, and given by the Johnson family to Chale Church in 1861? It must surely have been meant as a memorial to their great father Sir Henry Allen Johnson. To date, I cannot answer these questions, so if a reader knows, please contact the author!

(If a reader wishes to learn more about the history of Chale Church, a booklet is available in the church.)

Now with that preliminary to the talk on burial records, I shall attempt to portray the talk which looks at the humorous side of church burial records. For nearly 50 years the Churchyard itself has been maintained by a separate Committee, made up of representatives of various village organisations, including the Women's Institute, Parish Council, Parochial Church Council and the Horticultural Society, all of whom support the upkeep of God's Acre so generously. As its Chairman, I am proud of the way we are able to maintain such a large area, and to receive many compliments from visitors who come from all over the world. The church is indeed the dead-centre of the village.

It was quite common for such visitors to ask of those who might be working in the area, "can you tell us if, and where, our 'Great-great-.......' is buried?" Many of the older memorials have suffered the effects of weather and time and the wording can only be read at times of the day when the sun shines directly across the engraved lettering. Many do not have a memorial, and if they do, it can be difficult to find them. With this in mind, it was decided that the Churchyard Committee would aim to list all the names of those known to be buried there, as evidenced by the official church records. A copy may be bought by anyone who is interested.

Someone commented "that won't take long"!

Firstly the records, back to 1679, are kept in the Isle of Wight Record Office in Newport (for all to see). Armed with pencils (no pens there, please) and paper we went to spend a morning extracting the names! We were faced with the problem that without an authority signed by the Rector, we could not take details. Back home, another day, now armed with an authority, we started to look at 'our' records. There were four sets, the first two being joint registers covering Baptisms, Marriages, and

Burials, the other two having separate books for each occurrence. The trouble at first was that everything was so interesting that we spent much of the day just reading about all sorts of 'other' things these books contained.

Prior to September 1538 there was no requirement for recording burials. I suppose William I was the first to start recording things, with the Doomsday Book, and through the intervening years it was only important people; priests; Kings; leading Monks; etc. who would have any form of record kept, but on the Reformation, Henry VIII, and Archbishop Cranmer made orders that:-

"Item, That you, and every parson, vicar or curate within this diocese, shall for every church keep one book or register, wherein ye shall write the day and year of every wedding, christening and burying made within your Parish for your time, and so every man succeeding you likewise, and also there insert every person's name that shall be so wedded, christened or buried; and for the safe keeping of the same book, the Parish shall be bound to provide of their common charges one sure coffer with two locks and keys, whereof the one to remain with you, and the other with wardens of every such Parish, wherein the said book be laid up; which book you shall on every Sunday take forth, write and record in the same all the weddings, christenings, and buryings made the whole week before, and that done to lay the book in the said coffer as before; and for every time that the same shall be omitted, that party that shall be in fault thereof shall forfeit to the said church three shillings and four pence (forty pence), to be employed on the reparation of the said church."

The first books were to be in velum, but this was later reduced to 'good paper'. Some larger parishes used to record the details on a form of notebook and the information was later transcribed to the Registers.

The coffer is now often known as the Parish Chest; over the years the weekly recording of records fell to probably once every month, six months, or once a year in small parishes; and I doubt the fine was paid! What happened to the Chale records before 1679, if there were any, is unknown, but they do not now exist.

The two of us each took one book and decided the format we

would adopt to record the information. It soon became clear that there was a lot more information available than just names. The date of burial, christian name, surname, sometimes a house name where they lived (probably only for property owners, farmers, etc.), and age at death. However, in some cases vital information was missing – sometimes just a name and no date or age, sometimes just a surname, sometimes just a date and a dash. I can just see the priest and the 'warden', sitting at a table writing up the record. "That ol man who died last Michaelmas; wat were is name?" "Oh, can't remember. Put a dash an' we can fill it in later."

Indeed, perhaps the clue to the accuracy of these early books came at the start of the second, in 1699. With just the year recorded, the name is given as Thomas Green, followed by a short note as to his status; indeed, clearly an important man of the Parish – "Curate to Mr. Mitchell, who was Tutor to the Good Sir Robert Worsley – He kept the records 1679 – 1699 (very ill kept)". Indeed those words adequately described the first book; it was very ill kept! Thomas Green was in fact the Parish Clerk who would have been employed to write up many parish and church records, and possibly apart from the priest, would have been the only person in the village who could read or write.

What was also clear was that these joint records had to have been written up once a year. All the christening records came first, then all the marriages, followed by burials. A whole year's records of each, but no gaps.

The Parish Clerk was a very important person. An article in a Family Tree Magazine makes this clear. It records that the Parish Clerk often regarded himself – "Of great significance and yielding place to no-one in the parish, in regarding themselves as of no less importance than the parson". It also confirms that in many parishes he was the person responsible for entries in the registers, and his punctiliousness, or otherwise (our Thomas Green) depended on the accuracy of the records before Civil Registration was instituted in 1837. Between 1538 and 1837, the only place where burials are recorded is in the Church Records; after that date there are usually two sources of this information, the Church Records and the local authority.

The article continues stating that the Parish Clerk received a small remuneration for carrying out his duties which was sometimes supplemented with provisions such as eggs and flour. He might get in addition 13 shillings and 4 pence for looking after the church clock (often the only timepiece available to the poor members of the community). Also, four pence for every plough land throughout the parish, and for every cottage two pence paid annually at Easter. Also at Easter he might get two eggs for every Cock and for every Drake throughout the whole parish. (I can just see Thomas Green going round asking all the ladies how many Cocks and Drakes they had, collecting his eggs.) We have a connection here with eggs and Easter, albeit it probably originates in pagan times.

Further reference to the role of the Parish Clerk is that he would often lead the singing of hymns by reading out the words of one line and allowing the congregation to sing them, followed by the next line. It is said that in one parish the Clerk was so slow that a service would take all day, and the worshippers would even take snacks with them to stave off hunger, it took so long.

There are two further references to the Parish Clerk and it was clearly a job for life! One, Tristram Newman, is described as "The old honest Parish Clerk" when he died in 1767, and 49 years later, against William Cooper is recorded as having been the Parish Clerk for 49 years when he died in 1816. The name of Tristram Newman still survives in a road name in Chale to this day; his family having been land owners in the area. I can see him now dressed in a tricorn hat; a frock-tailed coat, breeches; buckled shoes; and a wooden staff, walking through the village greeting everyone he met. "How do, Tristram."

The church records were clearly used to note special events affecting the parish, often entered and signed by the Rector. One who made several entries was the Rev. Corbet Shelbery who entered details of beating the bounds. In 1735 he records that 60 of the inhabitants went with him round the Bounds (boundaries) of this parish. As Rector part of his income was from tithes and he needed to mark these boundaries to establish what was his by right. In 1755 he states that he "took a view of the lands belonging to the parish and went the boundaries of it from Watershoot" (near Blackgang/Rocken End on the coast) "to Snape End" (very close to where the Hoy Monument is now on St. Catherine's Down). Rev. Francis Worsley also recorded going round the Bounds of the Parish with 32 people named and listed in the book, in 1778, and just 7 people in 1792. (It would seem he also experienced some apathy with the Church as we see in the 21st century!)

Corbet Shelbery had a nice little earner in his family. In 1838 he buried his son in Chale, and in 1738 he records Mrs. Mary Pettit of London and adds "my wife's sister" and then signs the entry. In 1741 he buries his mother, described just as Mrs. Shelbery the elder!

The Rev. Corbet Shelbery was quite a lad. He was also Rector of St. Lawrence Church, as well as at Chale, although he lived in the Chale Parsonage. He was a keen fisherman, and one Sunday was busy mending his pots at home when a parishioner reminded him that he was supposed to be preaching at St. Lawrence that very day. He jumped on his horse and rode at speed over to the Undercliffe, and rushed into the church where his congregation was waiting. Sadly, he rose up when he should have ducked down and struck his head on the stone lintel over the doorway; and fell down stone dead! They buried him at St. Lawrence; later his tomb-shaped memorial over his grave was found to be in the way when they built an extension to the church, and rather than moving it, they simply built the extension on top of the memorial, trapped there to this very day! Part of the memorial is inside the church and part outside!

Another event was recorded in the Burial Record book by the Rev. Francis Worsley, a descendant of the Worsleys of Appledurcombe who was also Rector at Chale; the removal of the Chale parish gun in 1777.

"Lent to Sir Richard Worsley, Bart., one piece of Brass Ordnance belonging to the Parish with this inscription 'Anthony Bond made me' dated 1628. Sent by me in my cart to Appledurcombe with a carriage on two wheels and a bed from the gun, weak and worm-eaten, the wheels had a tire of iron", with the footnote:- "This piece of Brass Ordnance above mentioned was lent and sent to Sir Richard Worsley by the leave and consent of the Parishioners of

Chale". I feel he wanted to cover himself in case someone accused him of giving the parish gun to his uncle!

This was at the time of the American War of Independence and I think there may have been a call for as many guns as possible to fight the Americans, and Sir Richard Worsley was probably responsible for collecting them on the Isle of Wight.

Whilst mentioning Rev. Francis Worsley, there is a fine memorial to his son, Major General Sir Henry Worsley of the Bengal Army GCB who died in 1841 aged 73, on the wall beside the right hand altar. The inscription refers to "...ever ready to comfort the orphan and the widow..." and "...erected by those whom he affectioned, who esteemed his virtues, his friendship, and his worth". He seems to have been quite a popular chap!

It was about this time in our investigations that a prominent heading on one page broke the news that in 1752 the calendar as used most commonly in England – the Julian Calendar – changed to the Gregorian Calendar. Changes had been introduced from 1582 but it was not fully adopted by this country until 1752. Indeed, there have been continual changes worldwide over centuries, but it was the major change in 1752 which nearly ended our task of recording the burials in Chale! Very basically, prior to that year, the first month was March, and the last was February. Some month names were based on Latin, i.e. the eighth month had been October, 'oct' being Latin for '8', etc. and that is why February has 28 days, or 29 in a leap year (as the last month of the year). It clarified why in all the preceding pages, the monthly listings all started with March and ended in February. I should have known that, but it did not cross my mind. We had been using the numerical dating for our records, i.e. 10th January 1720 in the records was written down at 10.1.1720 whereas it should have been 10.11.1719! and that ignoring other minor changes. What should we do? It was agreed that if we started using that system, those who were searching for the ancestors who, say, had died in January 1720 would be totally confused if we showed 1719. Also, it would have conflicted with dates on headstone memorials of the time. So we said "bugger it", and left it as we had noted it, and continued with our work!

Some analysis of what we found indicated some interesting facts. Priests buried there included two Burleighs described as 'Clerk' in the records. A memorial on the south wall inside the church to Rev. Richard Burleigh and his wife clearly indicate that they are both buried 'near here', but there is no record of this in the Burial Records. The wife died first; was he too upset to write her in, or was it that they were both absent-minded as intimated by the scattered books engraved on the top of their memorial? Whatever, here is another indication that you cannot be certain of everything you see!

There are clear records of Chale residents attaining great ages with several over the age of 100. The oldest of whom was Margaret Howe who died in 1997 aged 107. The Burial Record proudly records that she was 'the Island's Oldest Resident'. In earlier years they were not so certain. When Robert Tutton was buried on 2nd December 1772, in the 'age' column is written 'A very old man'. I can see them contemplating this entry. "Ol Tutton, how old were 'e", "O, a very ol man!" John Spanner who died in 1809 is recorded as being 'Aged'; and George Chambers in 1754 was 98 years old. Life was precious, and when young James Roberts died (the twin brother of Edward) on 1st February 1924 his age is shown as 30 minutes!

The most predominant surname is Brown (mainly farmers in Chale) with 52 recorded; then Wheeler with 51; and Spanner (again farmers and landowners) with 50. My own family has only 39 recorded, but there were also several females buried whose names had changed on marriage.

Chale is not endowed with many famous burials, but the prominent 'Angel' monument records the Reade family who set up the Blackgang Mission. There is a railed grave of Lady Elizabeth Cole of Kensington who died in 1857 aged 79 years; and also of Christopher Smith, a founder of the Y.M.C.A. who died in 1892. The Rev. Constantine Sinclair, Rector from 1940, had a dislike of this organisation and wrote in the records, in pencil, "the chap who thought up the name Y.M.C.A."

But we do have an Old Goody Bagg there, in 1727, her christian name being clearly shown as 'Old Goody'.

One famous Rector often wrote 'died suddenly' against a name in the records, some who had died on holiday. George Weeks died suddenly visiting Shanklin in 1897, a warning to us all!

There are two men described as Private Centinels (soldiers) who died within a fortnight of each other in 1738. I wonder if they had a duel and shot each other! John Hillier, seaman of the Preventive Service (later Coast Guards) who was killed by a cliff fall at Atherfield, (did a smuggler push the rock?). Catherine Grapes, aged just 7, was accidentally burned to death in 1839, and Henry Spanner, aged 11, was accidentally shot with a gun by his brother in 1834.

A not uncommon death was by falling down a well, as did Elizabeth Russell in 1768. (I expect she was pulling up the bucket of water one wet day, slipped, and ….gone!) Even worse, perhaps, was Samuel Rooks, aged 18, who 'suffocated' in the well at Chale Parsonage in 1819; and Thomas Saunders 'supposed to be murdered' in 1747. And others.

There was a bit of luck for those left in Chale in 1894 when William and Esther Welstead both died 'of fever', and one of their nurses, a Nurse Chan, died also, at Ventnor, 'having taken the fever there'. Thanks Nurse Chan for taking it away from Chale!

But the following notes gave me much to laugh about when I came across them. I have a tendency to read something at the start and anticipate the ending. I read "…Killed with his mare under him…". Now that looked interesting! The whole entry referred to Robert Urry, aged 76, who died in 1745 "…with his mare under him, coming from Newport Market, by Emanuel Whites team of Sheep Wash…". Robert Urry was a Farmer and had presumably gone to Market; sold well and probably enjoyed a drink in Newport. As he was passing (by) Emanuel Whites sheep wash, the horse spooked, slipped and fell and Robert died. But where else would you find such a clear description of the incident! (I still think my first reaction was better.)

The reason for the death is rarely shown, with the exception of several cases of Small Pox around the period of 1750. I can only assume this is because there might be a risk of the Small Pox virus surviving in the ground, and if another grave was dug in the same area there might be a chance of spreading the germ.

I have been asked several times if a similar situation occurred with the Great Plague, but as this occurred in 1665, some 14 years before the Burial Book was started here, it would not show. In fact, the impact of the Great Plague on the Isle of Wight was not severe. Other plagues were earlier.

One fact which seems somewhat strange is that of all the various occupations shown in the Burial Records, there is not one described as a Fisherman, and that in a village adjoining the sea, and where most people would have had some connection with the fishing trade, Mackerel being the most popular fish to be caught there. I can only put this down to the fact that probably every fisherman was also a participant in the Cross Channel Trade or smuggling; but that would be kept secret. Smuggling of brandy went on in Chale for probably twenty years after it had stopped elsewhere on the Island! Probably the parson himself was a participant!

Whilst I am not prone to using swear words in my talks, occasionally they are appropriate! I feel that if they are used in the church Burial Records themselves by the Incumbent, I can be excused? If it is my friend the Rev. Corbet Shelbery (he who hit his head on the lintel at St. Lawrence Church) that's O.K. He used the term bastard several times!

One must remember that it is only the dead who are recorded here and only dead children, a fairly rare occurrence, would be classified as bastards. In the 21st century there might be more chance to use the term for birth out of wedlock, but thankfully few of these die! But in old Corbet's time (1745/70s) there seemed to be a lot of little bastards ending up in the Churchyard. Not only that, Corbet liked to name the offending parents whenever he knew who they were.

In 1745 little Hannah Sanders, the bastard of Rebecca Sanders was buried, and in 1748, Jenny Speed, bastard of William Speed and Jenny Blow died aged 3 weeks. In 1747 disaster befell the family of the old honest Parish Clerk, when Tristram Newman's daughter Ann had a son with John Spanner and this bastard was buried in the Churchyard. But perhaps the most worrying occurrence, however, was as recorded in December 1770 when two little bastards, - "of Mary Downer & - Green, a married man of Shorwell" were buried having died as infants within 10 days of each other; why we know not. But think of the shame it must have brought to Chale at the time – not just because he was a married man, but from Shorwell of all places. Godshill, or even Brighstone (Brixton at that time) I could accept, but a married man from Shorwell, oh dear, the shame of it. The fact that this detail is recorded indicates that it was a major sin to befall their dear mother! And Chale.

Death in the House of Industry (the Work House) is shown in several cases, and one of the benefactors who invested in its construction (and helped set up schooling in Chale) Robert Weekes is buried here. As were patients who ended up in the Lunatic Asylum (Whitecroft Hospital built around 1895). One, a Reuben Edmunds, was described (in a diary of the time) as having been taken there in 1916 when he started hitting his head with a hammer!

The Chale Poor House (located near Chale Church, and later burned down by Joe Bastiani after he had been evicted from there) is mentioned in 1772 when a man called Froyle "Died in the Poor House, crippled by a horse which he used inhumanly" (the spelling in the book). What did he do to the poor horse; what did the horse do to Froyle?? And in 1747 there is the burial of Elizabeth Wills, "a Parish Child".

Perhaps the greatest surprise was the vast amount of information given in the records about shipwrecks when drowned personnel were buried, mainly along the north wall near the famous Clarendon Hotel. Not only were the numerous names listed, but often from where they had originated, their age, and occasionally their role on the ship. The records also contain details of the incident, cargo, etc. For instance, with the wreck of the Clarendon in 1836, is written "… persons wrecked off Blackgang Chine on the morning of 11th October 1836 from the ship Clarendon, laden with rum, sugar, etc. and bound to London from the Island of St. Kitts. Out of a crew and passengers of 28 persons, 3 only were saved".

And of the Swedish Galliott 'Charles 11th' of 100 ton burthen, laden with fruit, which was unfortunately wrecked off Sandrock Spring Dispensary early on the morning of Christmas Day 1832. She struck and immediately went to pieces, the Captain, his son (aged 7), and Mate being drowned, the remainder of the crew, 4 in number, being saved. What an excellent source of facts for a researcher, but would you think of looking in the church Burial Records from such information?

But I usually end this talk on a matter which I entitle "The cunning of a woman!" I give verbatim what is written in the records of the burial. No name.

"The body of an unknown man was picked up off Blackgang, supposed to be about 30 years of age, and to have been in the sea about 6 weeks. 14th June 1869.

On 17th June this body was claimed as that of Hugh Lee, Able-Seaman who had been washed overboard from the RM Steamship ONEIDA off the Needles on 10th February 1869, (4 months before) by his widow who, on seeing in the newspaper a notice of the inquest held over this body at Chale, came here and called on me. (The Rector.) The clothes found on the body, which were in an unusually well preserved state," (if they had been in the water since February!) "led the widow to conclude that it was the body of her husband" (remember his body was buried three days before this). "The widow is residing at Southampton."

What the official outcome of this event was is not known, but at that time, a widow could not get any help or claim any entitlements unless a death certificate was produced or there was clear evidence of a husband's death. She might well have children, and they were probably penniless, and if she could persuade the Rector to give her a death certificate she could make a claim! This body was buried, and no longer recognisable; she probably thought – He will do" and made the journey to Chale to claim her fortune. Yes, the cunning of a woman!

A good place to end a talk!

CHAPTER 7

Self-Sufficiency
and Goat Keeping

I was quite young when I was born during a German bombing raid on Cowes, on Oak Apple Day in 1942. I arrived in what was later a Probation Office, but was then the 'Blue Ginnie' Nursing Home in Crocker Street, in Newport, Isle of Wight. I do not remember much about it.

Having survived the Second World War, my life was centered in Chale, on the Isle of Wight, where, in common with most children, I was encouraged to do all those things which are now frowned upon, or even illegal. I sometimes wonder how we survived. We collected birds' eggs, and became proficient at blowing the inside out to preserve them in our collections. By so doing we learned so much about nature; we could identify each species of bird from their colour and size, and also from the construction of their nests – now denied to the children of the 21st century.

We collected wild flowers, and we even had classes in the local Horticultural Show for named wild flowers. By so doing we learned about their names, their habitat, and their beauty. Cutting flowers rarely killed the plants themselves, and usually encouraged growth.

We were encouraged to cull vermin such as rats, mice, foxes and badgers; to kill rabbits not just to control their numbers but also to provide much needed food, and pelts. At an early age I knew how to paunch a rabbit, skin it, and prepare the carcass for the stew pot. Similarly with a hare, some varieties of bird including game, and even badger made good food. We picked mushrooms and learned which were good to eat or poisonous, and how to cook them when we got home after a forage.

We kept animals and birds; most homes in the country had a pigsty and one or two pigs who ate all the waste food from the kitchen and turned it into meat. Hens, ducks, and geese for eggs and meat; some even had 'Gleanies' (Guinea Fowl). These were named as they were proficient at picking up fallen grain following the harvest, so cleaning the ground of seed which otherwise would become weeds.

I recall we had two geese, given to my father, the Carrier, as payment for a delivery. One proved to be a runt and never grew; the other prospered until one day she got her head stuck in a baked bean can, and we had to cut her head off to save her life. At least she tasted good!

The garden itself produced most of the family's needs, the soil being enriched by manure from the pigs, and so we learned how to sow seeds and grow vegetables.

Perhaps all this automatic understanding of how life in the country, which was instilled in us from those early days, led automatically to what in the 1970s onwards became known as Self-Sufficiency. It is almost impossible to produce everything for a meal from one's own garden, but I did almost achieve it at least once with a meal of vegetables from our own garden, meat and gravy from a pig grown from our pigsty, (or was it meat from a goat, or a sheep?), and a pudding from fruit from the orchard. Salt, and sugar for the custard, may not have come from the garden!

I do, however, recall that the Government encouraged the growing of sugar beet just after the war, and many farmers took advantage of this new crop. On harvest they were piled up by the roadside from the field where they were grown, often with a large section of the natural field hedge being removed. These gaps remained for many years, but most have now been filled with new thorn hedge.

I also recall that a lot of homes in Chale, during and just after the war, grew and cured their own tobacco. From what I can find out, it is not illegal to grow and use tobacco for your own use on your own land; it is only if one tried to sell it that duty would become due. Many garden sheds would have the large broad leaves hung up to dry in the autumn. I believe they used them for either pipe smoking or to make a cigar type of smoke, or possibly to chew? This is no different from wine making which we do today for our own use.

The fact is that, shortly after my father's death and we moved to his home, a request was made "Let's get a goat". We had the land and we had sheds for housing, so that was not a plausible excuse to say "No". "You would have to have two" seemed a defence. "Yes" was the reply. "Where would we get them from?" "There are two advertised in the paper, only a mile or so away" "How would we transport them?" "Perhaps the man would bring them?"

With all chance of rejection quickly disappearing we arrived at Mr. Nunn's farm. "They will go in the back of your car, no problem". They did. A recently kidded, and milking female British Toggenburg and her kid.

We arrived home; set up a suitable stall with straw, etc., and then realised it was time to milk her! Never having done this before, it was a challenge. Indeed I think it took nearly an hour, and we still only had a cup full, but we could try it. It was delicious, so perhaps not so bad after all. The kid drank the rest. We were goatkeepers. In fact a photograph taken in the 1920s in the same garden here showed two fine female goats, so goats being kept here was nothing new! The difference was that in those days they were probably just a mixed breed or British; but still producing good milk, albeit sometimes rather 'strong' as the taste would often transfer from the herbage the goat had eaten.

As time went by, we became more proficient at milking, a skill which soon became automatic! We also learned about feeding and housing, often by trial and error. Tethering was clearly unsatisfactory unless one was on hand every hour to move them on, so open access to shelter proved more suitable.

By the end of the first summer, and the onset of autumn, the need to mate the goat and produce kids and milk for the following year posed itself. No major problem, as a return trip to see Mr. Nunn's stud male when the goat was in season, soon solved the problem. Five months later our first home-bred kids were born!

Soon after this, our first milker caught Entrotoxaemia and died rapidly, a most traumatic experience. I must admit I cried; perhaps as much because it indicated my failure as a goatkeeper as for the loss of the animal! This led to an urgent need for a replacement milker, and we acquired an old, white, lady, with a curled horn on the front of her head. Not much of a looker, but a good milker. She also proved successful at the following I.W. County Show; her confirmation was good!

In that second year we took our first British Toggenburg kid, now a goatling, to the I.W. County Show, and she won her class. I am not sure if that was good or not, but was perhaps to change our attitude to the whole game! There was an assumption that as we had won on the Isle of Wight, we could win anywhere. Some other exhibitors were taking their stock to England to show, Romsey being the most convenient; we decided to go too, after all, our goatling was a winner!

Whilst those with milking goats had to travel overnight and stay in the tent from before 6 o'clock the night before, we could travel on the morning of the show day, and so missed the early comments (and criticisms) of other exhibitors! We took our place in the class, and came last, of 17, and correctly so, when we saw what real quality animals looked like, in a national show environment, we were the poorest there. So that was the end of a bit of fun, or should we try and do better next time. This would involve buying in a quality animal from a top breeder on the mainland; not always easy!

Taking our young stock to what was known as a 'Kid Party' on the Island gave further encouragement to the showing game. It also gave the opportunity for human kids to show off their skills in a show ring with goat kids! Here the current year's goat kids were earmarked (with a tattoo number mark). These events proved very popular. It also enabled more people new to the game to meet each other and talk about their experiences.

We got new stock, and it led to us keeping the white 'British Saanan' breed. The most prolific breed on the Isle of Wight then was the Anglo Nubian, but they did not attract us. We wanted something different! One lovely British Alpine bought in from Devon never quite lived up to her expectations, and was eventually sold on, back to the mainland!

At first, the number of serious goatkeepers on the Isle of Wight was fairly small, and they were encouraged to join the Hampshire Goat Club (which covered the Isle of Wight) for help, pedigree registrations, and advice. However, as numbers expanded rapidly, there were enough members to justify a separate Isle of Wight Goat Club, and encouraged by the then leading B.G.S. judges, Paul and Betty Franche, our own Goat Club was formed, and eventually reached nearly 150 family members. I claim to be its first member (although someone else says they were first!).

In those days there was no restriction on selling milk to the public, or other goat products. Many people sold 'over the garden gate' and signs of 'Goat Milk for Sale' were common. That was before the Europeans got their little claws into British life and ruined it forever. I never heard of anyone dying from drinking raw goats' milk! The ability to sell your milk to a public who wanted it for health reasons meant that goatkeeping was economically viable. There was a time when I had nine goats in milk, and I was able to sell all the milk I produced, albeit being processed and bottled in the kitchen. The demand from parents with young children with health problems such as asthma, eczema, hyperactivity, etc., was enormous and I could not meet the demand. Even today I get people coming to me and saying that "my Mum bought goats' milk from you because I had …., where can I get it for my children!" Whilst goats' milk is sold extensively in supermarkets now, what people want is 'raw' milk, and they want to buy it from the farm gate.

There is a demand for milk to rear lambs, puppies, and other animals, which can be sold 'not for human consumption'.

This led to what became almost a joke! I was working in a Bank in Ryde, and had to get up by 5.30 a.m. every morning to milk, etc., before going to work. On the way I would deliver milk to a number of customers and then found that some wanted to collect it from me, in the Bank. I had people who would come in and go to the enquiries counter, ask for "… 2 pints please …" and go out. One day, a little old lady stood open mouthed watching this going on, and commented "I have never seen milk being sold in a Bank before!" and then adding "can I have some?" when I told her it was goats' milk! I only had enough to meet orders, so I could not supply her. I am sure there were Bank rules about such a practice and I am sure I should have been stopped, but no-one dared to do so. I visited our Area Office on the mainland one day, and saying from which branch I came, was told "… that's where they sell goats' milk isn't it …?" not knowing it was me who sold it. After a while I had to abandon the market when I reduced the herd considerably; there was just not enough time in the day to look after them properly. My other customers collected from the front door!

Returning to the show ring, it is here that one learns so much. I am so pleased that I was around at a time when the older brigade were still there. It probably goes back to the Second World War when most of the young men from farms were called up to serve leaving the farms to be run by sisters and wives. In many cases they were not able to milk large numbers of cows, and so the goat was an ideal substitute as the 'house cow'. Easy to milk, easy to manage, and produced enough milk for daily use. It also produced good meat for the table.

There are two main areas which bring back happy memories, although at times they were not always funny; the show ring, and stud males!

I showed goats with some of those famous names of the past, but their aura brought an element of fear when in the ring. I remember Mrs. Shields, a dominant lady who in the 1930s had fought the British Goat Society, and proved herself right, over the registration of polled male goats. The B.G.S. brought in a rule to only register naturally unhorned (polled) male goats to try and breed out horned goats. This proved disastrous, as most of their progeny were infertile. Mrs. Shields ignored the rule which meant that she could not register her goats in the Breed Herd Books, only in the Identification Register. She retained her blood lines which proved her to be right in the end.

I remember standing next to her in the ring at Romsey. The rule is – do as the judge says – but not Mrs. Shields. Her aim was to catch the judge's eye, so she did exactly the opposite to what the judge said! If he said "face your goat to the left", she faced to the right until he told her to change. She would stand two feet forward from the main line of goats being judged before being told to move back, grumbling that there was a hole where the judge wanted her to stand. "Face your goats towards me" was interpreted as "face their rear ends towards me", etc. He was in no doubt that Mrs. Shields was there, and inevitably she got the prize – because her goats were the best in any case!

Most of the leading showers were judges also, and one would be the judge one day and an exhibitor the next; they all knew each other, not someone like me, and they wanted to ensure they were seen before us mortals.

Another 'old' lady judge, a lovely old dear I am sure, was a Mrs. Payne. In judging goats every entry is placed, right down to last, so you knew which was the best and the worst. The judge would pass a brief comment about each one, from 'lovely goat' etc. for the winner, or a more chastising comment to the last! I took a white B.S. kid over to Romsey one year, and whilst I gave her a wash before leaving home the night before the show, she inevitably got slightly dirty by the next day. Where she should have been spotlessly white, she was frankly 'grey'. Alone OK, but against others, a poor comparison. A sponge over was of no effect.

Mrs. Payne made just three comments to me during the whole time we were in the ring; and it was the same single word each time – Persil! (It was at the time when Persil used an advertising gimmick of having two people wearing which shirts, one of which was not as white as the other.) At the first inspection she said, slowly, "Per-sil". When she called me forward for placing, instead of saying my number she said "PER-sil"; and when she made her comments in the final line (we were not last, but not far off) she said, slowly shaking her head "PERSIL", and she looked at me straight in the eye, and gave a little grin. I had to comment "I know what you mean, sorry!". She raised her eyes, grinned again, and I never spoke to her again, but I have never forgotten that day! She taught me a lesson (and Persil is very good to wash a white goat!).

In another year, I was at Romsey without a milker to show. The then BGS Chairman, Mr. Paul Franche (who had originally proposed our I.W. Goat Club) had four goats in the final line up, and as was quite normal, needed to ask someone else to take a goat of his into the ring. He had just one left, and I was probably the only person left with a white coat on. I was honoured that he should ask me to take his animal into the ring for him. They were all placed in order, and I was somewhere near the end of the line, but I did not worry as it was his 'worst', and would not have won a rosette in any case. When the judge got to me she stopped and said "Is that Paul's?". "Yes", said I. "I thought so, I should have known, I help him milk some times when he is away at a show; oh, you should be down there, say seventh". I was moved up about 10 places! Say no more.

I was fortunate enough to win the Best in Show award on several occasions on the Isle of Wight, and it was also an honour to be included in the full Grand Parade at the end of the Show, with other animals.

The breeding side of things is as important as any, and using a quality stud male will hopefully improve the stock for the future. To do so will often mean going to another breeder who has quality stock of your breed, or obtaining a male on loan from the mainland. I have been fortunate in being able to do the latter on several occasions, and you have a responsibility to look after these prized animals during their stay with you.

One fine British Saanen male I had on loan was Alpha Ambassador, from a good mainland line. He improved the white goats here for years to come. He was big and strong! He also had two problems which I was left to look after whilst with me – he had an ingrowing horn bud; and he had an udder! The first had followed disbudding and had left one horn growing back into his skull which required to be cut off every few weeks. This involved using a hacksaw. Whilst the horn itself has no nerves in it towards the outside end, the animal did not appreciate me sawing into his head! So it was two or three short quick stokes, and then try and remove the blade before it broke; it usually did.

The other problem, the udder, was not so easy, although not so dramatic. This sometimes happens in a high yielding strain of goat such as British Saanen; the udder produces some milk which must be eased out or mastitis may develop. The udder is next to the testicles, and often looks similar!! He did not take kindly to my delving amongst his goathood, but it had to be done, and every Saturday morning I ventured under his stinking belly to get a hold of his teat and squeeze out as much yellowy liquid as I could. I did not try drinking it! After a few weeks we got to know each other!

Sadly, whilst I carried out these duties as instructed regularly, I heard later that on his return home, the owner failed to do so. He developed mastitis, and died!

When Ambassador first arrived with me, I called a friend and suggested she come and look at him. She arrived shortly after, having had to go to hospital to have a plaster put on a broken leg earlier. Now, one of the traits of a male goat is that he will try and make himself smell as much as he can by spraying urine on his under belly and down his legs; that is why they do smell. He will also ejaculate over himself if he can! More pong!

When he saw this nice clean plaster cast on a leg, it proved too great an attraction and he immediately proceeded to mount my visitor's leg and spray the cast with both liquids – it had been some days since he had indulged. This stuff does not come off easily, even on one's hand it can prove difficult to completely wash it off, so there required a return visit to the hospital for the plaster to be changed, and an embarrassing explanation of how it had acquired its current extraordinary smell. Shall I say that I am reminded of this incident every time I see the person again, albeit years later.

The smell on the hand used to emerge whilst I was at work, even though it had been scrubbed rigorously. No-one ever said anything, but I did get some funny looks; or perhaps they thought that was my new aftershave!

Ambassador had another trait which was made worse because I had to go into his pen to feed him. He would usually be quietly resting, or asleep, in a corner, and I would place the feed in his bowl and escape before he rose. We got on really well, and indeed I could make him walk backwards (not an easy thing to do) by just looking him in the eye, and pointing my finger at him. Just occasionally he would jump up and try to butt me in the side. I usually parried the blow, but on one occasion I did not see him get up, and missed his lunge towards me. There was a large nail driven in the wall on which a bucket would hang, and he pushed me onto it. By luck (or otherwise) it missed me and passed between my legs (shall I say!) causing no pain, but I did not wait for more!

When serving a goat, I prefer that there are two people, one holding the female on a lead, and one holding the stud male, also on a lead. Ideally one lets them get to know each other for a minute or so before encouraging the act to take place. Sometimes he will need little encouragement and completes the task, the first time, very quickly. If, however, the female is not fully in season, the male will not want anything to do with her. On other occasions one lets them circle and 'fondle' each other. Ambassador was always as much interested in butting me first, so I had to keep a careful eye on him; we got on well, really! The procedure is repeated again a few minutes later, giving two services at a time.

But even a goat needs some rest, and normally two females in a day is enough to ensure a good, full, service to be successful. I would ask anyone who wanted to bring their female over to me to ring first. On my answerphone message I had the words "… if you want a service, please come after 5 o'clock …" which used to cause some hilarity for those who did not know what the message meant.

One Saturday a lady phoned to say she had two goats in season and could she bring them over. I said yes, but we would have to give him a rest between each one. She could leave them here and I would let her know when they were ready to return. Around mid-day, and I was watching snooker on the T.V., this lady arrived in my yard, with four goats in the back, all bleating away and wagging their tails furiously, indicating they were in season. "You said there were two" I commented, "but you have brought four!". "Yes, when I went out to get the first ones, I found they are all ready". I had to politely say that dear Ambassador, as strong as he was, could not cope with four in one day. "Oh, why not? I will leave them with you and call back later".

We installed all four and she left in her little car. I got one out, Ambassador did the job, and I returned indoors to see Steve Davis complete a frame of snooker. I then went out and brought out another female, and Ambassador served her. Remember I am having to hold both of them, alone! All O.K. so I went back to watch another Steve Davis frame. Those familiar with Steve will know he could be quite slow, so a frame with him was probably about half an hour. Then I served girl number three and returned again to the television. Then, after another frame, the last was served. The male goat was now taking longer to achieve a service, but he seemed still quite capable.

As mentioned, I try and give two services per visit, so there were still four more to come, and I repeated all four again. Each with a Steve Davis frame of snooker in between! After tea the lady returned for her goats quite unperturbed by her expectations of my male goat. She paid her fees, and dare I say, five months later they all kidded on the same day. So now, if I am ever asked how long does it take a male goat to recover between services, I simply say, as long as it takes Steve Davis to complete a frame of snooker – and as he gets older he seems to take longer!!

To animal keepers, the act of insemination is all part of the job, but to some it can prove a little too much to bear. One well known gentleman who had bought a couple of goats from me and looked after them well, brought one female to me to be served, having never had to do so before. I told him to hold onto her lead while I got the male out, only to find he had dropped the lead and had disappeared when I came back. Asking where he was, I heard a voice calling from behind the wall of the house saying he was "here". Asking why, he said he thought it not right to watch!

I did try taking two of my females to the mainland to be mated at different times, but the journey by ferry and road proved too much, and both were out of season by the time I arrived at my destination. I recall one elderly spinster lady, on seeing my girl simply saying "She's not in season; a waste of my time". Such is life!

On several occasions I made trips to the mainland, visiting other goatkeepers, sometimes for my own benefit, and sometimes to take other goatkeepers to mainland breeders to buy a kid, or just to visit. The most extraordinary was to a fine old Georgian mansion on the hills behind Honiton in Devon. This once majestic building had been left to fall into disrepair and there was a tree growing out through the roof in one area, and a water tank in the Hall to catch the rain as it came through the roof.

The house was full of remarkable antiques and paintings, and the owners lived in just some rooms which were not too badly affected. The lady had won championships with her goats at the Royal Shows after the war, and we stirred our tea with spoons awarded as prizes. I was encouraged to make use of the toilet, not for the relief, but to just see it. Having risked life and limb by climbing over the two broken treads at the base of the staircase, one entered an enormous room which housed a large bath in the centre, stained heavily with brown 'rust' half way up the sides. To one side there was what must have been a magnificent Victorian toilet resplendent with an ornate pull chain, and also the brown stain in the pan. Yes, I must say it was something out of this world.

Outside, the brother and sister who still lived in the family home, were converting an ornate Victorian horse stable block into a new residence for themselves, but had been held up by the swallows nesting. The stables had once housed horses, and they had bred thoroughbred racing horses to be sold on; had bred a Crufts' champion Cocker Spaniel; champion beef animals; had Ravens; and also British Alpine Goats. A breath of air from the past, sadly neglected.

It was pig slaughter day which always attracted some excitement. Whilst we could slaughter goats and sheep 'at home', pigs had to go off to the slaughter house due to the extra requirements of scalding, etc. I had also been brought up with pigs, usually two or four being kept at a time. There was a ready additional source of feed for them from stale bread collected from the Bakehouse on the Green, and being received in part payment for carriage of flour, etc., for the bakery. Barter was normal!

I can recall seeing a pig hanging in our shed following a home slaughter either just at the end of the war or shortly after, when the meat was preserved by salting in a large barrel. The hook on which the pig was hung up was still there in 2016! At that time pigs went to Flux at Wroxall to make into bacon (from a larger carcass than for pork); later they went for the smaller sized pork which could be killed at home. Even when quite young, my job of a Sunday morning was to 'muck out' the pigsty; removing the dung to the dung heap and taking out into the outside pen the clean bedding straw, and filling the bedding area with new clean straw. Pigs are most clean animals keeping their sleeping quarters dung free, and messing outside.

I also recall that at one time we used to allow the pigs to roam in the orchard whilst the sty was being mucked out, returning to their sty when all was ready. One day, when I went to call them back, they had gone! I called to my father, and he went off to find them, but they could not be seen anywhere, when all of a sudden all four came running home and went straight into their sty. It was not until a day later that we heard they had been seen making their way to Appleford; were turned round by someone on the road, and they made a return journey of probably half a mile, and through several gates, without stopping. They never had outings to the orchard again!

The removal of pigs to slaughter always meant the arrival of the chitterlings (small entrails of the pig's stomach) the next day, all of which had to be washed and cleaned of muck. This was achieved by turning them inside out, a skill one soon learned at an early age. They were then plaited into strings before cooking or frying; a lovely meal! We would also get an additional supply of chitterlings from some of my father's customers who gave us theirs in exchange for collecting their pork or bacon.

In the 1970s when our pigs went for slaughter they returned later when they were in half sides. A strong wooden bench was brought into the kitchen from the shed, and a local butcher would come and butcher the joints. Pre-arranged collections were made by friends and relatives who called to collect their share of the meat for an agreed price. The special smell of freshly slaughtered meat, and the taste of a special cut of meat cooked before being frozen, which filled the kitchen for days, added to the enjoyment of the event. The results of the pig rearing would be enjoyed for months to come, and the freezer was full again.

The rearing of sheep was similarly productive, but here we could slaughter in the garage. They also produced wool and the shearing was another special time of the year. I recall we had an open day here for the Goat Club when a local shearer did the job with hand shears in the old-fashioned way in front of an admiring audience.

Those special experiences of the popular self-sufficiency period have been regenerated in my life time due to keeping goats, a way of life few children will experience these days!

CHAPTER 8
Smuggling

I grew up in the knowledge that our family, the Sprake family from Chale, were involved in what I call the honourable trade of Smuggling.

Trade, because it was a question of buying the goods being smuggled into the Isle of Wight, or anywhere else around the shores of the United Kingdom, and selling them on, hopefully for a profit. That is trade. It was often referred to as the Cross Channel Trade; the Illicit Trade; or the Free Trade; but always a trade.

Honourable, because all the smugglers were doing was not paying the duty which was due on such goods; they were paying for it in hard earned money, mainly gold coins which were the basic currency of the time. Most duty and taxation for centuries imposed by the government, was used to fight wars, mainly with the Spanish or French. Nowadays most taxation (you might disagree) goes in supporting social benefits; but during the 1700s and 1800s, little was provided in the form of benefits to the poorer people. Yet they had large families and the opportunity to make a little extra income on the side from smuggling was almost a right which was eagerly sought. They were doing the best for their families; an honourable cause!

In a book which Jack Jones wrote about the Isle of Wight some years ago he refers to "... The parish of Chale was a smuggling centre in the opening years of the nineteenth century and benefited from the hidden income that came in. Here even farm labourers owned their own houses, an unknown situation in most rural parishes..." I have myself seen deeds of properties in Chale purchased by labourers, and with a mortgage, the labourer having been employed by our family.

We had been Mackerel fishermen from the mid-1700s, having our boathouses at Ladder Chine, a small windblown Chine between Blackgang Chine and Whale Chine, in Chale Bay. Here they kept their boats which could be rowed or sailed with a mast and sail. They had the ideal opportunity to cross over the English Channel and join in the lucrative trade.

By 1833 Robert Sprake had obtained a licence to brew beer, and also to sell such as wine, spirits, tobacco, snuff, perry, etc. which needed a licence at that time, from the Star Brewery at the top of Town Lane, in Chale. The family operated a brewery there for the next 100 years. They were able to smuggle in spirits (mainly brandy) and sell it over their bar counter, as well as elsewhere. They had the staff, employed with fishing, and also in the brewery, to ensure the success of the trade; they paid good wages, provided housing, and generally looked after their staff well; they in turn looked after the family's business interests! A nice little set up.

Smuggling involved goods on which duty was payable. For centuries, wool had been a major source of income for the British Government. Duty was payable on the export of high quality British wool, and often prohibited totally. The importance of wool is still demonstrated in that the Lord Chancellor sits on the

'Wool Sack' in the House of Lords. This provided an opportunity for wool to be taken to the Continent where it benefited from high prices, but more importantly could be used as 'currency' to buy spirits, wine, tobacco, tea, etc.; anything on which duty was payable. This enabled English (and Isle of Wight smugglers) to enjoy a double benefit from the trade.

There were several basic methods used. Each involved a group of people getting the funds together to buy the goods; sailing over to the Continent (prior to 1800 probably to the Channel Islands which were part of the British Crown, and where they enjoyed the benefits of having duty free ports). Going in the calmer weather of the late Spring or early Summer, in the dark, when a new moon gave less night time light, they would row or sail over to Guernsey or Jersey, a trip taking say 10 hours by going with the prevailing tides. They would buy the brandy in ½ anker tubs (about 4 gallons of neat brandy), tie them together in pairs and carry them down to their boats on a quiet beach; load the boats; and row back on the reverse tide.

Another method was to meet larger sailing smuggling boats and purchase goods in mid-channel, and return back to their home base.

On approaching the shore, signals would be made using spout lanterns (which could only be seen from immediately in front of the user) to indicate if it was safe to land; if the 'Coast was Clear'. If not, the tubs would be tied together, weighted down, and dropped just off-shore into the water to be retrieved a few days later. If all was clear, they would land, and the shore crew would assist in unloading the contraband from the boats, and stowing it away, in a haystack, barn, or even the Church! Otherwise, a few days later, they would return in their boats to search the sea bed with the aid of a 'peep-bucket', a glass bottomed bucket which enabled them to see what was beneath the water; and with a grapnel (a devise with a hook and pole or rope attached) pull the goods ashore.

But that was only part of the work. This was when the wives, or children got involved. The brandy had to be diluted to form a drinkable liquid, and increase the volume. This was usually done by the wives, often in a cellar, or under cover. They would burn sugar and mix it with water to produce a brown liquid which when mixed with the clear liquid of neat brandy, formed what was an acceptable drink of brandy in those days.

There were other methods. Whilst almost everyone was involved in the trade, there were those who sided with the Excise Men or Coastguards. They had to be kept 'happy' so to say. Behind the brewery at Chale there were pigsties. Brandy was often stored in pigsties, protected by a fierce pig, it would take a brave man to venture into a sty at night. Now, the Sprake family, so it is told, were generous to their friends, and also to the local 'law' who needed to be kept 'sweet'! They would leave an old used tub which had a small quantity of brandy in it, on the pigsty, and when the Coastguard came round he would take a welcome drink from the barrel saying what kind generous people the Sprake family were.

One day someone piddled in the barrel; the warmth of the liquid drew the taste of the brandy from the wooden barrel, and the result was a little more of the good stuff for our unsuspecting friend. He found more than usual in his tub that night, and drank it down with enthusiasm. Generosity comes in all forms!

The various people involved in a 'run' had to be paid. Whether you had put up the funds, were in the boat, part of the shore crew, the home workers, or moving it on and selling; all had to be rewarded, and as in any trade, the goods had to be sold.

There were many stories abounding about smugglers, such as the lady who, on seeing a Coastguard approaching her home, rushed upstairs and got into her bed. When he went to search her room she screamed as if in labour, and with her tummy 'full' under the bedclothes, her plight was one in which an honourable man would not wish to be involved. He turned away hiding his eyes and apologising for interrupting the lady. When he left she took the tub of brandy out from under her nightgown.

Another woman, working in the scullery doing the washing, sat on a stool with her crinoline dress reaching to the ground around her. Both the stool and the dress were hiding a trap door to the cellar below, where the brandy was stored. The story was that she was 'sat on the brandy', but these were small tubs, and she would have ended with 'piles' if she had sat there too long; what she was sitting over was the trap door leading to the brandy. She saved the day. On another occasion a young woman was seen hoeing turnips, and was sitting down resting when the Excise Man came along. Again her dress hid the 'stool' she was sitting on – a small tub of brandy. Even the often told stories of brandy, and smugglers, hiding in tombs in the churchyard were probably spread to keep people away from a churchyard which was surrounded in mystery. It was not unknown for a fresh grave to be dug somewhat larger than was actually required, and some tubs were hidden there to await removal at a later time.

Punishment if caught was often not as severe as if, for instance, you were caught stealing a sheep; remember sheep and wool were highly prized goods, and hanging could result if convicted. If as very occasionally happened, someone was killed accidentally, then the law had to be applied, but for smuggling a man might get a few months in jail or for repeated offences, perhaps a period of hard labour in the Navy. One such, a James Buckett of Brighstone, was at home on a ship, and his knowledge of local waters was quite valuable to a ship's Captain. James Buckett was eventually released after five years with an early discharge for good conduct.

Another punishment for a fisherman convicted of smuggling was to have his fishing boat cut in half, and they tended not to float very well after that. Their boat was probably the only source of income they had, and so this spelled disaster to him and his family.

He, as was the case of many smugglers, who were also fishermen, formed the crew of the early lifeboats with great distinction. I am often asked if the smugglers were 'wreckers'. My answer is no, certainly not in this part of the world. Their first concern was the saving of life at sea; but once the crew was safe, they would have made every effort to clean up any flotsam or wreckage left behind and a good living could be had in what might be described as salvage!

The other problem as far as the law was concerned was that nearly everyone on the Isle of Wight was involved in some way with the Free Trade; even the magistrates would have received rewards from the trade, and would not have done anything to spoil the source!

However, one famous name, that of William Arnold an energetic revenue officer, became Collector of Cowes. He was the father of Thomas Arnold, the future Headmaster of Rugby School. William did all he could to catch and stop smugglers. In those days it would appear he was treated as a self-employed person, gaining his reward from his success, and having to provide his own boats, and hire his own crews. It is recorded that in 1781 he requisitioned stout, strong, four feet long 'tucksticks' to assist his officers in finding contraband concealed under the shingles on the beach, or in sand, or in cellars. Rather like a sword stick, it housed a long metal pole with a sharp point which was used to prod the area. Similar sticks, often called prod-sticks were used by the coastguard service for many years.

The name of William Arnold is recorded in Cowes High Street with a plaque which is there to this day. His problem was that even men he hired were themselves often regular smugglers!

The importance of the role William Arnold played in the history of smuggling on the Isle of Wight cannot be overstated. He was one of the most respected Customs Collectors in Britain, and was involved with developing the law against the trade, and yet in many ways his hands were tied. In the book 'At War With The Smugglers' by his descendant Rear Admiral D. Arnold-Forster, it is clear he knew all the local smugglers and their vessels, indeed he seemed to know when they were being built. However, in a way he encouraged the success of the smugglers. His vessels tried to stop the trade at sea and indeed they had Letters of Marque issued by the Crown authorising them to stop and plunder trading vessels of the smugglers and of enemy countries, particularly of France. As such they had the same powers as Privateers, basically private licensed pirates, and to get their reward they had to sell the plundered cargoes, through their own markets.

William Arnold's records around 1790 noted a great advance in the price of spirits in Europe due to the Napoleonic Wars which forced smugglers from other European countries to switch their trade to the Channel Islands, and Guernsey in particular which further advanced the illicit trade in those Islands. He comments that the high prices hit Isle of Wight smugglers particularly badly.

He recorded:-

"The Smugglers in and about the Isle of Wight were not supposed to be men of much property, (we have always been poor!), and many got into debt with their Channel Island merchants, and they had difficulty in getting credit. Because of this, when they were able to purchase goods, they often found it to be of inferior quality or short measure. Indeed the safe sure place to buy their spirits and tobacco was through the Customs House Sales market, where as Arnold says "at our sales they pay for no more than they have …" . Because of this the price of some spirits rose 100% from 4/- or 4/6d a gallon to 9/- a gallon in a year!

The Customs House Sales were selling goods they had plundered from smugglers, to smugglers, and making a good profit from it! The complexity of the subject is too great for this talk and I would suggest you get a copy of Arnold's book from the Library and see for yourself.

A short talk cannot give a full picture of what has become part of our heritage over centuries, but I aim to give a brief summary.

Most records show that brandy was smuggled from France in the 19th century. However, as mentioned above, the Channel Islands were almost certainly a regular source until around 1800. Prior to that St. Peter Port in Guernsey and St. Hellier in Jersey were regular destinations for our smugglers. However, throughout the 18th century the British Government tried to stop the trade through the Channel Islands, and on several occasions tried to set up Customs Houses in these towns, much to the annoyance of their residents. Many Channel Islanders relied on the smuggling trade to survive; for instance at one time, over 700 people were engaged in Guernsey as Coopers (making barrels of all sizes) for the Illicit Trade. Ending of the trade would have brought financial disaster to them and the Islands.

Towards the end of the 1700s, Napoleon enticed the south coast smugglers from England to purchase their goods through ports in France, and made them into Free Ports. Not only did France benefit from the increased trade, but Napoleon was also able to gain valuable information about the British Navy from visiting fishermen. Other laws affecting the Cross Channel trade came into effect around 1800, and in 1808 one of the first Chamber of Commerce was established in Guernsey (also in Jersey, and earlier, I understand, in Aberdeen, affecting the smuggling trade from Scandinavian ports). In visiting the Guernsey Archives some years ago I came across the first Charter forming the Chamber of Commerce there, signed by numerous merchants in the town; I have a copy (with their permission) of the original. The wording states –

"We the undersigned merchants of Guernsey, taking into consideration the critical state of the Island and the necessity there is for taking steps to preserve the few channels of trade left open to us, have resolved to write and form a Chamber of Commerce for the purpose of concerting together on the means best adapted for the purpose – and think it desirable in the first instance to declare our resolution not to carry on from this said Island directly or indirectly any illicit trade with the Mother country, but on the contrary to assist with all our power in the execution of the Laws and Ordinances passed for its suppression, and further that the undersigned by admitted as a member, but will previously agree to sign a declaration and give his word to the same effect."

That basically ended the 'lawful' smuggling from the Islands, and from then on and throughout the 19th century we traded with French ports; our family using Roscoff as their main port for future trading.

Throughout the 19th century the Sprake family were never caught, I can only presume their generosity in its various forms helped protect them. (Someone once asked me if I had their account books; I don't think they kept any, do you?)

My own Great-grandfather, Charles Sprake, as the eldest of the third generation brewers, had a leading role in the business, and even as a teenager was entrusted with the knowledge of the trade, almost unheard of for one so young in those days. Whilst still young, his job one dark night, was to rake over the marks left by the keel of the boats, and the foot prints of the crew, having landed a cargo. His face was blackened, and his collar turned up to hide his features, when along came the Coastguard. It was not unusual for a fisherman to be on the beach late at night, but they approached Charlie and asked him if he had seen anyone there that night? With forethought, he said "Yes", he had. "Which way did they go?" "That way" he replied, pointing in the opposite direction to which they had gone. The Coastguards ran off, in the wrong direction, and the family trade was saved. Safe in his young hands.

But, as with everything which seems to be going too well, disaster struck when he was just 29 years old. Having been on a fishing trip with two friends, the sail got stuck up the mast, and one of the crew climbed up the mast to free it. The boat, called "The Spider", which had a reputation of being unstable owing to having been tarred too many times, capsized. All three were thrown into the sea. The others grasped the boat, but Charlie drowned; as a letter at the time stated: "His washing was in the sea"!

That was the end of the Sprake involvement in the smuggling trade. The rest, as they say, is history, and another talk!

I once gave this talk to a group of school children who had been primed in the unsavoury nature of smuggling. They say never act with animals and children! At the end of my talk to them, one little girl, looking very serious, asked "Isn't smuggling illegal"? I could only reply with the word "Yes"!

Whilst not strictly smuggling, these three family letters written at the time of Charlie's drowning interest my audience, and demonstrate how life was in Victorian times:-

"My dear Cousin,
Oh how can I write and relate to you such a sad sad accident of my own dear brother C. He went to Freshwater yesterday with Mackerel in their boat. There were three of them, Alfred Spanner, Charles Chick, and poor dear Charlie, and when they were coming home from there about a mile from Freshwater, they were putting up the sail, and it was not quite right, and Spanner got up on the mast and over balanced

the boat and upset it and they were all thrown out into the
water, and they sank and rose three times and the last time the
other two grasped the boat, but poor C is gone, and his poor
washing in the sea. Oh, poor Alice (his wife) is almost Wild
and her three dear little children, and poor Mother and Father,
I am afraid they wont be able to bear up against it. Oh such a
blow to us all, dear Cousin.

    I cannot write more, with kindest love to you,
        Your affectionate Cousin, Alice Sprake

                              Monday"

On 15th June 1873

"My dear Cousin,
    I suppose you heard the news. I wrote a letter to you
yesterday directly I heard the news of poor Charlie being
picked up and gave it to Father to post, and he was so upset
that he forgot it and we did not know until this morning.
    Tuesday – I was so sorry. The poor boy was picked up at
Compton Bay yesterday, Monday, about a quarter past one
in the afternoon and Mr. Murrow of Freshwater Gate Hotel
went and telegraphed as soon as he heard it (no mobile phones
then!) and we received the telegram in about 2 hours after, it
was so very kind of him and soon after that the Coastguard
that picked him up came to us and told us all he could (I
expect he was the one who used to have a swig of brandy from
the barrel on the pigsty), and the man that drove him, Oscar
(her brother) told them when he was there he would satisfy
them (give them a tip) if they would keep in strict watch
for him, but they were not willing to take anything for their
trouble (no, no, Charlie was a good friend we would not take
money...) but Father gave them a half sovereign each (a lot of
money for the time, I expect they said, Thank e very much, Sir,
any time he dies we will do ar bit).
    The poor boy was found with all his clothes on the same as
he went down in and the money and two knives in his pocket.
Oscar went there last night, and John Linington (a close family

friend and relative, and an undertaker) with him, and the Shell (a temporary coffin) and when they got there he was put in one. Mr. Saunders, a carpenter made a coffin and put him in it and he was laid in his workshop, which was very kind, but took him out of that and put him in the other which was lined all comfortable and they put his shirt on the best manner they could, Oscar took his hand and straitened all his fingers, excepting the one that was crooked that gathered that time; he said the rest part of his body was the same as ever excepting his features, and they were altered (he had been in the sea for 10 days).

It was almost 3 o'clock this morning before they got home and we went to bed and we are now waiting for his poor body to be brought. It's now almost midnight, we were prepared, the bearers and all at 4 o'clock this afternoon but to our great disappointment we received a note by the Coach (stage coach) to say the inquest could not be held until 8 o'clock tonight so that it will be morning before they will get here. Poor Oscar will be almost worn out, I am afraid he is gone again today, he has a great part of it on his mind, but the Rev. Theobald was kind enough to say that he would bury him so it's proposed to be done about 11 o'clock tomorrow morning if possible. Dear Cousin, we shall now know where his poor body rests which will be one great relief to us all. It seems to renew the grief again. Father is very poorly, and so is Mother, his appetite is so bad. Alice (the widow) is as well as we can expect; she came up today expecting to see them arrive but poor boy he will be missed by many. I am writing tonight as I cannot do much else and it passes the time (there is nothing much on the tele). He will be laid in old James Saunders house just below us tonight (he worked for us, and bought his house, with a Mortgage, but lost it as he did not keep up the repayments) it's empty and it will be much better there.

Fanny and Mary and Sarah came on Sunday to see us. Poor Aunt is very poorly Sarah said, also poor Aunt Anne I am sorry to say is not so well, poor thing. I hope you are well, we should have expected you if the letter had not been mislaid, but as it is it cannot be. I must now conclude with all our kindest love to you.

   I remain, Your affectionate Cousin, Alice Sprake"

"Wednesday, dawn.

Dear Cousin,

 I have just finished clearing up. The poor boy was buried this morning, soon after 11 o'clock we all went to look at his coffin this morning but we were not allowed to see more.

 I hope now we have seen the worst. I am sorry to say that Mrs. Woodford at Bearley (near Niton) is dead. She died yesterday morning, they said she was almost mad and barked like a dog before she died. We began washing Monday and went through it once and it has not been touched since for Mrs. Woodford (that's Mrs. Woodford who barked like a dog's daughter, and she does our washing) was obliged to be called away Monday, but I daresay we shall get through it alright. I must now say Good-bye, the post will soon be leaving, please write as soon as you have time.

   Alice"

CHAPTER 9

A Century of Sports and Games in Chale

From time to time I am asked to put on an exhibition in Chale related to village activities; and am also often asked questions about where sporting events took place, and when? This usually by 'overners' who find it hard to believe that Chale once offered so much in the way of sports. In July 2017 I was responsible for an exhibition which was mainly prompted by enquiries such as "… where was that …?", or "… when was that …?". They do not always believe me, but where doubt exists I try to prove my answer by artefacts, press cuttings, or trophies.

"Where WAS Chale Golf Club, then?" usually followed by a tale of the Chale Golf Club. To those of us of ageing years, the answer is simple, "… on the Down!". I recall when young that the Club House (which still exists in the trees at the back of the so-called View Point Car Park on the New Road from Chale to Niton) was visible for miles when coming up the Military Road from Brighstone. On the roof of the building was, prominently painted in white, CHALE GOLF CLUB, still resplendent years after the Club was closed due to the effect of coastal erosion, and Adolf Hitler.

The Chale Golf Club was set up around 1900 under the enthusiasm of Henry Way, of Pyle Manor, Chale, who was known as 'the Squire of Chale' and who remained the Club's Chairman throughout its existence. Also, at the end of the 1890s, Tom Roberts who had taken over the Clarendon Hotel (now the Wight Mouse Inn) was turning his establishment into a high class hotel attracting titled clientele including the King and Queen of Spain, and other influential customers. Just as hotel establishments these days often provide golf courses and tennis courts for the benefit of their visitors, so Tom, with the help of Mr. Way and his associates, was responsible for establishing a golf course on Chale Down (St. Catherine's Down). The first tee, and the last green, were roughly where the View Point Car Park now is. The course took players up to the Chantry (Pepper Pot) and around the open down land and back to the last hole. It was a 9 hole course, played as an 18 hole course by going round twice.

Chale resident, Fred Mew (author of 'Back of the Wight') was the Professional and also the Groundsman; other staff to maintain the course were probably just casual labour of which there were many (between farm work, mackerel fishing, and the occasional smuggling run!).

Press records indicate regular matches with both male and female golfers enjoying the sport. Whilst the Great War interrupted play, it soon expanded after the war and Chale Golf Club prospered until the disastrous cliff fall of 1928 blocked the main road from Chale to Ventnor, through Blackgang, forcing traffic for Niton and Ventnor to pass through Chale Green. In 1933 a new road (called New Road, although I am unaware that this road has ever been marked with this name) was created right through the first fairway. This did not stop play, even though golfers had to drive over the new road, whilst cars drove along it!

Many competitions were staged on the Course, sometimes attracting national and international players, and the Club, and Chale with it, prospered (as did the Clarendon which provided accommodation for visiting sportsmen, and no doubt the Press).

Then WW2 started, and the Isle of Wight was often subject to stray bombs being dropped by German aircraft on their way home from raids on Portsmouth and Southampton. In 1940 two such bombs were dropped beside the first hole, and the craters formed can still be seen on the left hand side of the main road near Blackgang. Just a half hour or so before the event, a courting couple had been sitting on the stile beside the road, and one bomb destroyed their 'canoodling perch'. It not only ended their fun, but the Golf Club was never opened again after the war.

It is always a joy to trace original items from past events, and thanks to the generosity of Tony Gazzard, the Island's golf historian from Sandown we had a lady's golf bag from the 1920s, three clubs, two with the name of Fred Mew, Chale, engraved on the club heads, two 'wrist score cards' (tiny printed cards fitted to a leather strap to record the player's score, hole by hole; the opponent's score; and the difference per hole). I assume these scores would be transferred to the official score card at the end of the round or just used for non-competitive rounds. A small silver trophy from Chale Golf Club awarded in 1930 for Mixed Foursomes was also lent to us.

Chale used to have its very own cricket field, still known to older residents as 'Cricket Pitch', although now some 80% of the field has been lost to coastal erosion. Originally known as Nodes, situated along the lane at the end of The Terrace, leading to the old Sandpit, and behind Cliff Terrace, it was a strange W-shaped field of about 5 acres, the shape presumably adding to the challenges of the game. Several of the players lived in Cliff Terrace adjacent to the field. Members of the Wheeler fishermen family were prominent, including John Henry Washer (whose mother was a Wheeler) who was the only Chale player to score a century there with 100 not out (including 3 sixes and 12 fours), around 1900.

Here again, it was regularly played on until the start of WW1, but after the war it became a hay field for Henry Roberts or for crops of Mangles (cattle fodder), although it was still called 'Cricket Pitch'. Matches were played there against teams from all over the Island.

Later, various fields around the village were used for cricket matches, although one in particular, on land attached to Westside Farm had to be abandoned as the balls were regularly being hit into adjoining ditches and too often lost. In 1950 the Rev. Sinclair, Rector of Chale tried to reform a Cricket Club, to play in his own 'Rectory Field' opposite the Old Rectory, but his appeal for bats and other equipment (with woodworms acceptable) or generous donations of £5, did not meet with much enthusiasm.

When I mention that a Regatta was held on the beach near to Rocken End (under Blackgang Chine) in 1909, 1910 and 1911, it usually brings exclamations of surprise, and some disbelief. We had several photographs of these events, and the large numbers of people present on the beach indicates the event's popularity. Swimming, rowing and related races were held, but the one which causes most amusement is the 'Dogs Race'. Clearly dogs were taken out on the sea in boats a short distance offshore, and then thrown into the water and encouraged by their owners on the beach, the first one to 'land' was the winner! What would the RSPCA say about that now? It may be interesting that sport of a different type takes place along this beach now, some 100 or more years later, as it is where naturists practice their 'sunbathing'.

Prizes were usually presented on 'Cricket Pitch' a few days later when singing and other entertainment was provided by local girls. In 1909 a concert by a visiting YMCA from Woolwich organised the event. Press reports at the time indicated well respected names such as Dabell, Pinnock, Roberts and Henry Way were prominent.

The Regatta may have resulted from a move in 1905 by the local County Council to encourage swimming lessons to be arranged through the local school. With the Chale beach area being unsuitable for teaching swimming, Mr. Harvey, farmer at Chale Farm, generously offered to allow swimming lessons to be held in his Sheep Wash, and the Council even agreed to pay 10/- for the pond to be cleaned for the purpose.

In the 1970s a Chale Swimming Club was formed, based at the School, although they made use of the pool at Brighstone Holiday Camp. Many school children from Chale learned to swim there, but it ended when the Camp burned down!

A full programme of Athletic Sports was first held in Chale in 1914, but the onset of the Great War halted that until 1919 when the Chale Sports Club held Peace Sports on the field opposite Chale Rectory, to celebrate the end of hostilities. The event concluded with a bonfire and a huge pyrotechnic display on the Down with flares left over from the war lighting up the whole village, albeit held three days later due to bad weather.

The pre-1980s period saw regular events which are banned these days, such as Fox Hunting, Beagles and Hare Coursing. Regular meets on the Green, or at The Clarendon, attracted large crowds and were regarded as part of rural life. I spent many Saturday afternoons when aged around 8 to 10 years, walking up to ten miles at a time with Greyhounds; my father's cousin, Tom Sprake, being the Master of the I.W. Coursing Club. I learned so much about the countryside from those wonderful years. A large gathering of members held the first meet after the war at Beckfield Cross, near Kingston. Tom Sprake won many awards with his Greyhounds, both at Coursing (hunting hares) and on the track, and a cup awarded by the I.W. County Coursing Club in 1932 was displayed at the exhibition.

Organised by the I.W. Hunt, Point-to-Point races were a feature of many venues in or near Chale, often changing from one year to the next. True Point-to-Point races were over various types of ground, including some ploughed land, some grass, and jumps were often just hedges or over ditches. The competitors could take their own route from one point to the next, originally from one church steeple to the next. After WW2, from 1949, Harold Linington of Atherfield Farm had a grass race track with jumps around his farmland which proved very popular.

As a young boy I was thrilled at the chance of attending the annual event with my father. Not a betting man, he allowed himself some latitude on Point-to-Point day, and would aim to meet a well-known local farmer who 'knew' the horses. He would get the name of the anticipated winner and place his small bet to add to the excitement. Some horses ran for several years in a row, and one which I well recall was Tudor Arch, owned by Harry Rayner from Chine Farm, who lived there with Arthur Jones. Tudor Arch usually ran in the Ladies Race, and was usually a safe bet!

The Parade Ring, etc., was in the field on the seaward side of the Military Road, north-west of Whale Chine, and the track was in the fields on the other side of the road. A good view of events could be had by standing on the mounds in the field beside the road. I well remember one year, having placed his bet, my father and I went and stood to watch the race and we found ourselves next to a scruffy individual who had been enjoying too much alcohol, and was sitting on the ground, unable to stand. He named a horse who he said would win, and it happened to be 'our' selection. There were just three horses in the race. Our horse took a steady start but fell at the first jump. Our intoxicated friend remarked "E'll win"! I was told to keep away from our new neighbour!

However, that left just two horses who made good progress with one nearly a full fence ahead of his rival. At the last jump, the leader fell, leaving just one horse in the race. "E'll win" insisted our drunken friend. Slowly the remaining horse reached the last fence with just one to jump, and he also fell. The excitement in the large crowd of spectators grew to a crescendo; the jockey on the first horse to fall, seeing his opportunity decided to proceed around the track. "E'll win". The other two had been dismounted and were making their way 'home'. Our horse by now was just one fence from victory; he sprang with enthusiasm at the last obstacle, and fell! He did not just fall, he lay flat out on the ground, winded, and some thought even dead. "E'll win".

Eventually, realising there were no more horses left in the race, our horse was persuaded to get up, the jockey remounted, just about got over the last jump, and with the jockey just laying across his saddle, made a slow but determined journey to the winning post. The crowds were cheering louder and louder. "E'll win" was by now prone on the ground and could not see what was happening. And "E" did win. I can still hear those cheers. "I said e would win"! What an end to a day's racing.

The other event I recall from many, was when Harold Linington had a horse running; which had been brought up going round this course on his owner's land. In his race, he fell at the jump right outside his owner's farm, and raced off by himself. After searching for the loose horse, someone decided to look in its home stable, and there he was, enjoying a nice rest in the straw!

Amongst various photographs I have of old Point-to-Point races in Chale over many years, it had been suggested one was of races at Southdown (between Pyle and the Military Road), but I could never establish where that was until I was shown a County Press cutting and report of races at Pyle Farm in 1927, with two wonderful photographs of the event there. It was clearly a very wet day, and a panoramic view of the event showed a large attendance of very 'posh' vehicles such as Rolls Royce, etc., with one badly stuck in the mud and being pulled out by two horses, watched by a gathering of spectators, including the local policeman. Another shows people pushing a beautiful vehicle out of the mud. The report of the event indicates that the elite of the Island were there, but not one picture of the races, just cars stuck in the mud. If those cars were around today they would be worth millions!

My father, Arthur Sprake, the local Carrier, was a successful athlete in the 1920s. In WW1 he served in the Army in South Africa, India, the Middle East, Turkey and Greece, much of this time seems to have been spent playing football, rugby and other sports!

On his return to the Isle of Wight in 1920 he took over the family Carriers business, bought a Model T Ford van and was the sole driver so his availability was paramount. To take part in amateur athletics events he had to join an athletics club and compete under AAA rules. He joined the Newport Trojans Club, and he soon became the Island Champion at Pole Jump, jumping with a solid ash pole with a spike in the end, landing on the hard ground with just a sprinkle of sand to fall on. He was never beaten. Due to an error by the Trojan's Secretary in filling in an entry form for a handicap event in 1924, he was suspended by the AAA from competing for over two years. Once reinstated he continued to win many trophies, and prizes like cutlery, silver coffee pots and ink stands. They were not allowed to win cash prizes as an amateur. Prizes for athletic events were often displayed in the County Press window before an event, so a competitor could decide which he wanted to win. If his selected prize was awarded to, say, the second in a race, you had to try and come second!

In the 1927 Isle of Wight Championships at the Recreation Ground in Newport, he won the gold medal for the Pole Jump, jumping 10' 3" and to show how high he could jump, he had the cross bar put on the top of the uprights, and still jumped some 6" above the maximum height. At home he jumped 11' 0", landing on the hard ground. His father feared he might injure himself and be unable to work. When Arthur was selected to represent Hampshire in the Inter County Games in London, his father hid the invitation until after the event was over, so he never took part. I believe the man who did go in his place won the event jumping 9' 6".

Arthur usually jumped wearing his flat cap! He rarely trained with his Club; his only training was to jump all his customers' gates delivering goods to their homes, or in a field behind his house. He occasionally played football for Chale and took part in an exhibition match after the end of WW2 when an 'old Chale' team played a 'young Chale team'. His running spikes hung in his shed for over 50 years, and survive to this day, almost 100 years old.

Sport in our village was not just for men, indeed women have taken a lead in many events over the years. Golf was a leading sport as has been mentioned and I have a photograph of a ladies' team on the links with a trophy. The Chale W.I. had a successful darts team and in 1987 they won the West Wight final and qualified for the all Island final. Darts had been played in their Hall at Chale ever since it was built in 1911, and the original metal 'oche' or toe-line a player must stand behind is still fixed to the floor in their Hall.

The W.I. Hall was originally the Chale Working Men's Conservative Club, and then the Chale Men's Club. They always had a billiards table there for both billiards and snooker. During that time the Rector of Chale, Rev. Newhouse, presented a trophy for their annual snooker competition, and this was competed for until the early 1950s when the Club folded, and the Hall was given to the Chale Women's Institute. In approximately 2008, Chale Churchyard Committee started holding twice yearly Quiz Evenings in the Hall, and this cup was obtained and returned to the Hall and is now competed for every six months, and has been engraved as the Late Noel Turner Memorial Trophy. Noel was the Quiz Master for some 9 years until his untimely death.

Football was a prominent sport in Chale for many years, and after WW2 the then Chale team were successful in Island League matches. In the early 1950s they were rarely beaten. They played on several fields but the field opposite the house called Nightingales between Fullford and The Old Rectory was used for several years. I recall my father would park his van in the road overlooking the pitch and we could watch the matches in relative comfort whatever the weather. There is not room to include everything here, but one star of that team was Rudie Ratje, a German POW who had married a Chale girl and lived here for the rest of his life. By reputation he might well have achieved national recognition for the German football team if the war had not taken place. Rudie could play anywhere on the field, and often took several positions in the same match. Whether in goal, as an outfield player, taking penalties, or just passing the ball, he was magic. I personally recall he was in goal one day when a penalty was awarded against Chale. The referee placed the ball on a dubious penalty spot (the field was grazed by cows during the week, and they left their mark on the turf!). Rudie stepped forward and moved the ball slightly to one side and walked slowly backwards into his goal mouth. The opposition player moved the ball back, and Rudie then returned it to where he felt the ball should be. Where the referee was I do not recall, but this happened about eight times until the kick was taken, and the ball flew skywards over the bar! On another occasion the Chale team was awarded a penalty, the ball was placed on the spot, and Rudie who was the Chale goalkeeper was selected to take the kick. He ran, full pelt up the pitch and by the time he got to the ball he was at top speed. He kicked the ball with his usual accuracy and the goalkeeper dived to stop the ball, but the strength of the shot hitting his outstretched hands, dislocated several fingers, but the ball ended in the net!

My other recollection around that time was when Chale was in an Island League Cup final played at Newport's Church Litten ground. To Chale it was like playing at Wembley. The then landlord at the Clarendon, Major Cullen, was a leading supporter (possibly an officer of the Club). The Major, a stocky gentleman had a booming deep voice, and he spent the whole match calling out "Come On ChAAAAAle". Chale scored in the first few minutes, and led for most of the match, but with just a minute or so to play, the opposition scored and the result was a draw 1 – 1. By this time the whole crowd was echoing the Major's battle cry and the words "Come On ChAAAAAle" remained in our heads for weeks to come.

Ladies football is now taking a leading role worldwide, but at one time it was frowned upon, and I am told, any connection with male players was banned.

In 1970 Chale and local villages set up ladies' teams to raise money for local charities. In 1969, Hughie Green, the well-known personality who was promoting 'Opportunity Knocks' on television, aimed to get local ladies' teams to compete in Butlin's Holiday Camps, with the team winning the English division playing the Scottish champions in a final which would be shown on television. A personal letter exists from Hughie Green setting out his plans for the event.

In 1970 a team called Chale Wasps played football against Niton Dollies on Chale School pitch; two more matches between these young ladies followed shortly after, one at Chale and one at Niton. A further team named 'Wittul Wonders' was formed. Under the inspiration of Edwin Cole from Chale, who acted as trainer and coach, it was decided to pick the best of these three teams for the Hughie Green contest to represent the Isle of Wight, and they were named the Niton Dollies. In the first year they went to Minehead and won their match against Foden Ladies, and the following year they played at Minehead again, winning against a team from Liskeard in Cornwall, and then Clacton, where they eventually got beaten. The trip to Clacton involved travel on the London Underground, which for some was quite an adventure!

Another sport at which Chale residents excelled was badminton. There was a badminton court in the School Hall at Chale, and members of the Greville and Morey families were very successful for several years in events all over the Island.

Horticultural Shows, or Flower Shows as they were often called, always had sports, and in Chale the Show started as an athletic event. Variety events included obstacle races, and fancy dress races, often with men, usually village 'dignitaries', resplendent in female attire. Perhaps that was the origin of 'Drag races'?

One feature of athletic events at village shows was always The Mile Race, and this still exists today. Chale has a silver trophy which is awarded to the winner of The Mile Race every year, and the start of the last lap is traditionally signalled by the ringing of a bell. I recall in the 1950s one local competitor, Jim Richards, a local fisherman from Atherfield Coastguard Cottages, was a regular competitor and frequent winner. On one occasion he was asked to take part in a challenge race with Jim Peters, the English World Marathon Record Holder and Champion at long distance racing.

Jim Richards told me himself that the race was along the Undercliffe and ended in Ventnor Park; I do not know the actual distance. Jim Peters gave the other competitors a lengthy start, as he was 'unbeatable'. Approaching the Park, Jim Richards went further ahead at great speed, and Jim Peters could not catch him. He was quite annoyed as he was not there to be beaten; Jim Richards had not read the script. Peters asked Richards how he was so competitive; where he trained; etc.? As Jim Richards said to me, he ran every day along the beach from Atherfield Point to Rocken End and back, some four or more miles over the shingle beach which was very tiring. Most people could not last more than 100 yards there. When he ran on a grass track, or on the road, it was so easy for him. I am not sure if he told Jim Peters his secret!

Jim Richards was also a member of the Life Saving crew, and once won a special award for saving the lives of two women from a yacht in the sea off Niton. All this and he had been shot in the eye by a pellet from an air rifle as a boy, and had lost the eye.

Whilst mentioning awards, a small medal, won by Lewis Whittington early in the last century for shooting, was on display. I am led to understand there was a rifle range somewhere in the Blackgang area at one time.

I have in my possession a large box full of steel quoits, of different sizes, sadly now very rusty. Some of these have been 'restored' by a kind gentleman. Quoits, with metal rings, is still a popular pub sport in some parts today, but is more often played by children with rubber or rope rings. Where did they come from? I have no idea, but may well have been played at the Star Inn when it was part of our family's Star Brewery.

Pub games have always been popular, and many different games were featured over the years. Darts has already been mentioned. Dominoes is popular, but from comments made, dominoes with up to 9 x 9 dots (rather than the more usual 6 x 6 dots) was played in Chale. Rings is still played regularly, and Chale has for a long time had a successful Rings team and play in the Ventnor Rings League. Mainly an Irish game, it is Kent and the Isle of Wight where it is still played in England.

Pool is still popular in local pubs, and competitions often have cups and trophies for the winners.

Motor sports have been competed in by Chale residents, and the Sheath family at Chale Service Station won many Banger and Grass Track races both on the Island and the mainland thirty or so years ago. Diane won the National Grass Track Racing trophy amongst her successes. I am also told that in the early 1950s motor bike races were held with competitors racing down Gotten Lane, up Newman Lane, out to Westside and on to a finish. How 'official' this was I do not know, but no doubt it would be banned these days?

It was not just motor sports at which the Sheath family competed. Keven, Diane's brother, took part in marathons, and completed the London Marathon on at least three occasions.

Apart from the odd pub game, there are now no sports played in Chale, a village which once led the Island, if not often the nation at their chosen sport. No football team (although there is a pitch on the Recreation Ground); no cricket team; other than the Mile Race and some children's races at Chale Show, no athletics events; no golf club; no horse racing; etc. So why is this? It is easy to blame the dominance of television, the mobile phone, text messages and all the other devices which younger people worship these days. A major influence was unquestionably the closure of our village school several years ago which has wrecked the interest in active participation in sport. As to the future, who knows? Perhaps the resurrection of a golf club on the Down; a football team; and a cricket team, would be a start. We can only pray!

CHAPTER 10

Seager Wheeler – Wheat King Of The World

Many Islanders have made a major impression on their fellow citizens, both local and global, but few can claim to have had such an international influence as Seager Wheeler. Born in what can be called humble conditions, near Blackgang in Chale on the Isle of Wight, on 3rd January 1868, on the same day as his mother's grandmother; he was to take the rather unusual Christian name from her surname, Sarah Seager. It was her 101st birthday! And she had predicted that the new baby would be a boy, and be born on her birthday. Well, I suppose it was a 50/50 chance it would be a boy! But he did achieve the same date.

Seager was the 3rd child of Henry Wheeler and his wife Mary. However, the marriage was to last only another two years, when

Mary Wheeler ended it. Henry had an affair with a local woman, Louisa Chiverton, described as a housekeeper, and fathering young Ernest Wheeler, (and several others), who was perhaps to become the best known of all the Chale fishermen Wheelers. Mary decided enough was enough, and moved back to her family home in Ventnor, with her 4 children, to live with her mother. She took up work as a laundress, and later moved on to live at 28 Albert Street, Ventnor.

Some years ago now, the well-known Wheeler family historian, Mr. Danny Wheeler came to live near me in Chale, and casually asked one day if I knew of 'Seager'. My immediate reaction was "… what, the Wheat King of the World?" I think Danny was probably a little surprised to know that I had heard of his relative. I had good reason to know that name; it had got me into trouble when I was little more than 7 or 8 years old, and a good 'box round the ears' when I did not even know that I had done anything wrong; is an event one never forgets.

You see, it was like this. My father, the local Carrier and furniture remover, had been moving furniture for Mrs. Dot Harris (Ernie Wheeler's daughter) who was moving into the Post Office, and taking up the position of the Chale Post Mistress. She was the niece of said Seager Wheeler. I recall that my father came home with a small cardboard box containing a number of brown envelopes with 'Victorian' style writing on the front, with what I was told were the names of varieties of 'wheat seed' which had won Seager Wheeler the title of 'Wheat King' on no fewer than 5 occasions.

I asked my father if he knew Seager Wheeler, and he told me he had met him; he lived in Canada by then "… and he was Wheat King of the World? …" I enquired. At that early age I did not know what that meant, but suffice to say MY Dad had actually met a King! And not just any old King; I had heard of King George but he was only King of England and the Empire, but Seager Wheeler was King of the WORLD, And even more so, my Dad knew him. Was I proud? You bet I was. And this King of the World had got the title by sowing some of the very seeds which were in the brown envelopes.

The following spring, I had been helping my father to sow seeds in our garden, and I thought that, just perhaps, if I sowed these seeds, I too could become 'Wheat King of the World'? Perhaps it was like my very own 'Jack and the Beanstalk'. And that was when I made a very stupid move; to do something without asking first. I can even to this day remember that I waited until my mother was busy, and got out a rake and line (just as we had done a few days before) and marked out some rows to take the famous seeds. My next mistake was to sow them in exactly the same place as the lettuce and carrots…

The wait 'till Dad came home was long. Would he be proud of me; 'course he would! "Look Dad what I have done" Well, I can still feel the weight of his hand across my ears. I leave the rest to your imagination! I resolved never to plant anything again in the (b….y) stupid garden. This King business was not for me.

Over many years I often thought about those seeds; of Seager Wheeler; and was he really a King of the World? I never heard further mention of his strange name until that day when Danny Wheeler spoke to me. Even more interesting, Danny had a draft of a small book written by Elizabeth, Seager's youngest daughter, about his life; "Would I like to read it?" he enquired.

Well, that was a chance too good to miss, and I at last learned about this wonderful man, who had come from Chale to indeed become 'Wheat King of the World', not once, but five times! I looked forward to seeing the completed book in due course.

Some years after this, I had the privilege of showing a descendant of another Chale resident who had gone to Canada before the Great War, round our Church and Churchyard. We also went and looked at their former family (Harvey's) home at Chale Abbey. As I and Mrs. Jean Thompson were walking along I asked from which part of Canada she came and she said 'Saskatchewan'. I commented that there used to be a man who was born in Chale, just along the road, and who went to Canada and became the 'Wheat King of the World', who went to Saskatchewan. Without hesitation she said "Seager Wheeler". I was somewhat surprised that she would know of him. She said she worked for the Saskatchewan Tourist Board, and one of their most popular attractions was the Seager

Wheeler National Historic Site, in Rosthern (Seager Wheeler's former farm and home). "It is one of the most popular visitor attractions in Canada!" she said.

This encouraged me to look up Seager Wheeler on the internet (a dangerous thing to do!) where he has prominent sites. There was reference to a recent book, 'Canada's Wheat King', the Life & Times of Seager Wheeler by Jim Shilliday. Recently (in 2015) I received a letter from Elizabeth Wheeler in which she spoke of her father in devoted terms, and commented on the Shilliday book. She did not like it and considered it too 'academic', and 'he made too many assumptions'! I obtained a copy and it was clearly based on Seager's daughter's draft which Danny had showed me some years previously, and much more. With this information I was able to develop another talk which I felt would interest islanders and visitors alike!

But back to Seager's childhood, in Ventnor. He attended the National Schools in Ventnor where he was mentioned in dispatches. The Ventnor Historical Society (and their researcher, the late Fay Brown) were able to provide some snippets from their archives.

When 9 years of age, the School Log Book recorded that Seager Wheeler was ordered to be caned on the hand for 'repeated disobedience', and he was told to hold out his hand to receive his punishment. At first he refused to do so, so he was brought to the front of the class and caned across the back. Seager asserted that he would kick the Master 'and he threw himself on the ground, kicking and yelling vigorously'. Soon after, his mother entered the School and insultingly demanded her boy. She took him to the Vicar, and asserted that the Master had thrown the boy to the ground and held him down on his stomach whilst he flogged him. 'The true facts were related to the Vicar by the Master in the evening, who promised to see the woman again about her untruths'.

In May of the same year, there were a number of boys playing on a piece of land in Hamborough Road opposite the Vicarage (later the site of the Winter Gardens). Seager was with them and tried climbing the cliff which overhung the road, but was unable to reach the grassed area at the top. His companions (it is said in fun!) pushed him several times, forcing him to release his grip and to fall some 20ft onto the road below, breaking both his arms and being severely shaken. Life was not easy in those early days but prepared him for an even harder life to come.

Seager left school at the age of 11 years. His great wish was to join the navy. He had been born overlooking the sea, and he wanted to work at sea. Initially he took work wherever he could find it, doing gardening work, and odd jobs to earn some money. He also famously took work with W.H. Smith's book stall, and delivered newspapers around Ventnor. This was to prompt a headline in the I.W. County Press newspaper when he visited England in 1936 – 'Island Newsboy became Wheat King!' He joined the Naval Cadets as he felt an early training with the Cadets would give him a better chance of a career in the Navy. He applied several times but each time he was turned down because he was too small – he was told "… up and down you are an inch short, and round and about there is another inch missing …" He must have been shorter than 4'10" high at age 15 as this was the minimum height for sailors in the Navy.

Seager, his brother Percy, and friends were not averse to helping themselves to fruit from orchards, and on one occasion they were caught and spent the night in the local jail. What good it did them I do not know!

At home he was particularly close to Percy, and his sisters. They had an uncle who was farming in the Canadian prairies and he wrote to Mary Wheeler and suggested the family go for a year to Canada. "There were opportunities for young boys there". He had done similarly for another relative earlier. So, in 1885, when Seager was aged 17 years, the family left Ventnor and Seager got his longed for voyage to Canada. His great adventure in life had begun!

Even to get to their relatives' farm involved a five day trek in covered wagons, passing through Winnipeg and eventually getting to the uncle's farm at Moose Jaw Creek. Seager recalled that they saw many 'Red Indian' villages with wigwams, etc., and he lived the life he was taught about back in school at Ventnor. At Moose Jaw Creek, Mary Wheeler made friends with a Native American lady who had fallen into poverty. She had been the wife of the famous Sitting Bull, who had been responsible for the massacre of General Custer's army at the battle of Little Big Horn in 1876. For a young boy, albeit now a man, these were exciting times indeed!

Seager took work wherever he could get it, and worked for the Canadian Pacific Railway, doing anything to raise money for his future plans in agriculture. He also worked on his uncle's farm, including harvesting grain with a sickle, and threshing using a flail during the winter.

He and Percy worked for a year with his uncle cutting the 'first sod' on virgin land. Then he joined a construction gang of the Canadian Pacific Railway and worked for them for a year, including unloading cars of coal. They had been granted rights to most of the land in Canada and were responsible for opening up the prairies and selling on the farm lands, and in return transported its produce, grain, etc., to the ports for sale.

In 1890 Seager and his mother took over a quarter section of prairie land in Saskatchewan, renting from the Canadian Pacific Railway. This is a standard land measurement in North America, and measuring ½ mile on each side (a quarter of a square mile or 160 acres – well, that's what the web site says!). After two years hard work, Seager and his family had saved enough money to enable them to buy a small farm, and with a loan of Can. $200 from the Canadian Pacific Railway they bought wagons, oxen, and supplies for the onward journey to the west.

The journey proved treacherous, often contesting with severe weather and almost impossible land routes, over rivers and other obstacles. But eventually they reached their new home where Seager built the family a log cabin made from timber cut on their own land. Food was plentiful with Geese and Prairie Chicken shot on their land, and fish caught in their river, and with crops grown on their own land. They cut their first sod here and started to plough with oxen, and in 1891 when still just 23 years old, Seager Wheeler, from the Isle of Wight, was a Canadian prairie farmer.

But it was not easy, and the weather conditions meant that the growing season was short, and it was vital for the crop to ripen before the severe frosts and snow came. It was at this time he made contact with a Dr. William Saunders who was producing new strains of wheat to help withstand the severe weather, and he obtained some of his seed wheat. He also started to buy in seed grain through another relative in Australia. It was to set him on course to become the 'Wheat King of the World' !

His continuing search for better growing conditions led to the family making a further move to Rosthern, in Saskatchewan, which was to become his home for the rest of his working life. He had to borrow Can. $10 from the Canadian Pacific Railway for the first year's rent. Again he 'cut the first sod' and built his family a new house on the land and named it Maple Grove Farm.

1901 brought further disasters when an early frost caused the entire crop of wheat to fail and the grain did not ripen. In one great attempt to improve the strains he commenced selecting seed for the coming season by hand, using just a lantern and candle light. His selections were vital, but by 1904 just three years later he was producing 60 bushels of wheat to the acre, an almost unheard of yield in those days. Two of his original varieties of wheat included Kitchener, and Red Bobs, which led on to his famous Marquis Wheat.

Seager saw this seed selection, which covered other varieties of food production, as a way to make a good living. Indeed, in 1908, when aged 40 years, he married his wife Lilian. He started sowing his personal varieties of wheat. But life was hard and they were always short of money.

Marquis was proving the most successful, and he was by now producing 82 bushels to the acre. This grain proved highly suitable for bread flour; it had a strong upright stem and the head was also upright. Indeed, it stood almost to Seager's shoulders if photographs mean anything (but he was only short!!). This enabled the Marquis to withstand extremes of weather including the severe hail storms which befell the area.

By this time, Seager's brother Percy had also established his farm nearby, but he concentrated on work as an engineer. He built an improved 'Fanning Mill' or grain dryer, and Seager took his grain to Percy to dry. Percy also made a gramophone with an enormous horn. He built it outside, and found it too big to get indoors, so the two brothers enjoyed it by playing records in the fields where they worked!

Seager had taken an active part in local Growers organisations for some years, and in 1911, the Saskatchewan Grain Growers offered a prize of Can. $100 for wheat, which he won. At the same time the Canadian Pacific Railway Company were offering a prize of U.S. $1,000 in New York for the best wheat seed, but it was only open to U.S. farmers; Canadian's were excluded! There were many protests from Canadian growers, and they opened the competition to Canadians, and the S.G.G. persuaded Seager to enter with his variety – the Marquis.

Late in the night of 5th November 1911, Seager and his wife had been contemplating their future. The $100 prize had been useful, but his continual experiments with wheat was not bringing in enough money. There was heavy snow afoot, when at 11 o'clock there was a knock on the front door. He went down to see what had brought someone out in such weather, to find it was a telegram boy with the news that Seager had won the U.S. $1,000 prize (in gold) in New York, and he was now the first 'WHEAT KING OF THE WORLD'.

"Astounding" – his word, not mine! His shock soon gave way to the realisation that with the Canadian Pacific Railway's prize money he was now able to pay off what he owed the Canadian Pacific Railway Company! He had been almost constantly broke since he had gone to Canada. He now had money in the Bank, no debts, and he could continue with his experimental work.

The following morning a crowd of men arrived in his farmyard having stormed up the road in sleighs, pulled by horses. They included some of the leading members of the Rosthern community, all had come to greet their new 'King'. The Prime Minister of Canada also went there to congratulate Seager. It is recorded that they picked up the grinning 'monarch', his pipe clenched tightly in his mouth, and carried him shoulder high round the yard, laughing, singing and cheering. 'He had brought honour and recognition to them, to Rosthern, to Saskatchewan, and to the whole of Canada'.

One of Seager's daughters, tiny May, watched from the doorway of their home, and cried. She thought they were taking her daddy away!

The prize of 1,000 dollars in gold in a special case was presented to Seager in Calgary, and to return to Rosthern, Seager put the gold coins in a bag and hung it from his belt inside his trousers! The coins were replaced by cardboard effigies for display in the case.

In the following years, until 1918, Seager continued to develop his Marquis strains of wheat, and there was a demand from all over America and eventually worldwide. He entered the competition four more times, winning each time, being the World Wheat King on five occasions, a record which was never beaten. In 1918 he retired from competition. He faced the ravages of the extreme weather, and in two seasons hail storms destroyed most wheat crops in the area, but the stature of his Marquis withstood the first, and although a second was destroyed by hail, he had enough seed stored in his barns to continue the strains the following season.

His farming methods were in great demand worldwide, and he published a book entitled 'Profitable Grain Growing', and others. According to Elizabeth her father was extremely generous. He never sold any of his books, but gave them away to customers who bought a certain quantity of seeds from him. The role played by Dr. Saunders in the Canadian wheat production is acknowledged as significant, but it was our Seager Wheeler, the little boy from the Isle of Wight, that established Canada as the 'bread-basket of the world'; a term regularly used when I was at school.

In 1920, when 52 years old, the Queens University in Kingston, Ontario, conferred on Seager the honorary degree of Doctor of Law in recognition of the great work he had done in promoting the scientific side of agriculture. He had added enormously to the wealth of Canada, and every settler gained by his research. It was felt that on no-one could the LL.D. degree be more fittingly bestowed than on Seager Wheeler, and the degree was the highest honour that it was in the power of the University to grant.

He was now Dr. Seager Wheeler, LL.D.

However, the world became in turmoil with the onslaught of The Great War, and after the end of the war the Canadian Government decreed that the sale of wheat had to be centralised, and was being run by the Saskatchewan Grain Growers Association which prevented Seager selling directly to his customers.

Whilst he continued to produce and develop his wheat, he had other fingers in pies. He grew barley, oats, and other grains, and he started to produce fruit trees. He had his own catalogue and was selling some 60 varieties of apple, 80 of crabapple, hundreds of varieties of plumbs, raspberries and other small soft fruits, sunflowers, potatoes (varieties such as 'Gold Nugget' and 'Wheeler's Red') and even rhubarb. In every case he aimed to produce varieties which would withstand the vast changes in temperature and weather conditions common in Canada. He was able to bud between 300 and 400 fruit tree buds a day, in season.

He built further barns and storage units, a second house, and later a third, for his family all on his farm at Maple Grove Farm. And he always bought the best quality suits from London. Seager was a gentleman; Seager was a King!

Further acknowledgment of his success came in 1935, when aged 67, he received the King George V's Silver Jubilee Medal awarded to citizens for outstanding accomplishments. It was then that Seager Wheeler decided to make his first and only return visit to his homeland. He returned to the Isle of Wight with his family in 1935 and the Isle of Wight County Press newspaper headlined – 'Seager Wheeler Comes Home', 'Island Newsboy Became Wheat King', 'The Island is Indeed Proud of its Native Son'. The news also spread to national papers in England, one of which described him as 'Wheeler the Conqueror'.

Initially he spent three days in Chale staying with members of his Wheeler family, but then travelled around England where he met up with other relatives. He was pursued by the national press wherever he went. The King had returned! This publicity produced a number of letters from people claiming to be related to Seager, no doubt hoping for a share of his fortunes! Several weeks later he returned for a longer stay on the Isle of Wight. He brought with him samples of his famous wheat seed – which was the very seed which I lost in my garden as a child. Oh, silly boy!

His business and reputation spread, and continued into the Second World War. In the 1943 Honours List, King George VI awarded Seager an M.B.E., appropriate in that he was a citizen of the British Empire as it was then. The little newsboy from the Isle of Wight was now Dr. Seager Wheeler, M.B.E., LL.D., but more so he was the Wheat King of the World. He was always in demand for lectures throughout Canada and in the U.S.A. He was now 75 years old, but 1943 was to see the end of his illustrious career when disaster struck.

In the depth of winter 1943, nature which had co-operated with Seager for more than a half century as a silent partner, turned on him with wrath. Temperatures in Rosthern fell to minus 67°F (and that's 100° of frost – and a bit chilly!), freezing the trees' inner wood.

That Spring he found that most of his fruit trees had been mortally wounded. Those that survived fruited only on the new bark for a year or so, and then died. He had some 60 acres of fruit trees under cultivation which he had been developing for more than 30 years, and which had survived drought and depression, all wiped out in just one vicious winter. He decided he was too old to start planting new orchards again, and retired.

For many years he had had a keen interest in what was described as 'clean sport', including hockey and baseball, and the Rosthern ice hockey team took the name of 'The Wheat Kings' in his honour.

Even so he was still in demand as a lecturer and public speaker. He had been a life-long pipe smoker, and even when speaking rarely stopped talking long enough to allow him to light his pipe with a match which would often burn his fingers before he got the pipe alight! His friends and colleagues gave him a retirement banquet, and one made the following comments which must speak for themselves:-

"Dr. Wheeler was always a charming conversationalist, and when the topic was one in which he was vitally interested, his enthusiasm knew no bounds. At such times it was always a source of unalloyed pleasure to us to see him try to light his pipe. He would light a match and hold it to his pipe, but could not stop talking long enough to take more than one or two hasty draws. Of course, nothing happened and he had to drop the match to avoid burning his fingers. The same thing occurred again and again, and all the time we were laughing more at his performance than at the ready wit and enthusiasm of the great man."

When Seager rose to thank the friend, his eyes twinkled as he drew out his famous pipe, tamped the tobacco with his finger, and then held a new lighter to it, drawing out clouds of smoke which surrounded his head.

He moved to live out his illustrious life at Vancouver on the Canadian west coast in sight of the sea he was born to love, but following his death his remains were returned to Rosthern where a Salvation Army service was held for him in the Evangelical United Brethren Church, and they are buried in the rural Bergthal Cemetery there.

The home he built at Rosthern, Maple Grove Farm, is now a National Historic Site and operated by the Seager Wheeler Farm Historic Society, and I am sure he would be proud to know his work is still recognised.

But the Isle of Wight, and Ventnor and Chale in particular should be proud of their famous son who became the Wheat King of the World. I was asked once if one of the famous blue plaques noting the birth places of famous people might be erected on his former home, but that has long gone 'over the cliff' as we tend to say. Nature has sadly caused its own havoc. But I often think, if only I had kept those little brown envelopes, with samples of the wheat seeds which he brought home, I could stand and say, here is something of his life which made him famous. But I can't – I sowed them in the wrong place and still recall the box round the ears. There may be one last legacy however, my mother was born a Wheeler (albeit not of the same family), and so I can say I too am partly a Wheeler!

My grateful thanks go to Elizabeth Wheeler, Seager's youngest daughter who died in 2017 in Rosthern, Canada; to Danny Wheeler; and to Margaret Shaw, who have so kindly provided me with personal memorabilia of a great man whose father ran off with Mrs. Chiverton; who left school at 11; and who became 'Wheat King of the World'. Elizabeth wrote of her father ".. he was an Englishman to the end. I once told him he was now a Canadian, but he replied "Oh No! I was born an Englishman and I shall die an Englishman". He was so humble, and had such a childlike nature".

I also quote from a poem Elizabeth wrote lovingly of her father:-

"House-wifely proud the busy waves
   twice daily wash their floor
Of things the sea no longer wants
   and hurls them on the shore.

My father, then, he and his chums
   would search expectantly,
in hope of finding gold perhaps,
   long lost in storms at sea.

My father came from fisher-folk,
   the sea was in his blood;
his days were spent "down top 'o shore"
   or roaming Pelham's Wood.

His constant chatter, I am told,
   was going to sea when grown;
he'd man a ship that he would buy
   with money of his own.

But other hands were beckoning
   with tantalising voice
The sea? The land? Which should it be?
   God made for him the choice.

He loved the land, the grassy plain,
   the sky that touched the ground;
the prairie rose, the cactus bloom,
   the newness all around.

But still the Island and the sea
   were never far from mind;
the cliffs he climbed, the pranks he played
   with chums he left behind.

He'd hold his audiences wreathed in smiles,
   (those twinkling eyes of blue!)
when talking of his boyhood days -
   the dialect slipping through . . .

'Twas memories, cherished, stamped as firm
   as treasure on a chart,
that kept the boy, still anchored deep
   within the old man's heart."

And to quote his own words – "The soil is ours to make and
mar and we should aim to leave it, when the time comes for us to
pass it on – in a good or better condition than when it came into
our hand."

CHAPTER 11
Anecdotes

I have enjoyed giving talks to many different groups of people for nearly 20 years, and I get as much enjoyment from it as I hope my audiences do. I often learn things from them, and it all shows that they too are gaining from the experience. Sometimes the comments which come from the audience have no connection with the subject I have been talking about, so I include some of those little gems which I have gathered over the years.

There are times when someone asks a question and for some reason I cannot for the life of me remember what a particular word means. I recall when I first published 'Put Out The Flag', I was asked to have an interview on BBC Radio Solent to talk about my book. This was a great opportunity, and I had the choice of doing an interview on the telephone from home, or going to their studios in Southampton. I immediately chose the latter and I looked forward to the broadcast with excitement and some trepidation!

I arrived at the studio and was told I was being interviewed by none other than Peter White. There was no real preparation for the broadcast, so I waited in the foyer and watched as familiar faces came and went. Eventually I was taken into the studio where Peter, who has been blind since birth, greeted me by moving towards me and holding out his hand to shake mine. All sense of his disability disappeared and he indicated for me to sit down and put on the earphones. A lady sat looking through a window at what was going on. I had jotted down some basic notes just in case I dried up. Peter placed a Braille machine on the desk in front of himself, and started to ask me some questions as he jotted down my comments on the machine. Peter said he would like me to give a few anecdotes to add to the interest of the story I had written. At that moment I could not think what an anecdote was; one of those moments your mind goes blank. So I thought to myself, oh, I will give him a few stories, that will do. Later I thought about it and realised that that is what an anecdote is! He put me at ease, and we awaited the ending of the music which was playing, and he introduced me over the air. That's when things suddenly went wrong.

At the time I used spectacles to read, and I took them out of the case. The problem was that they had one lens which occasionally came loose. Yes, as I put them on my nose, it fell out; not just onto the table, but onto the floor, and under my chair. Peter was, of course, oblivious of my plight and proceeded with the opening – "Derek Sprake from the Isle of Wight has written …" I am now searching on the floor for my lens. I looked towards the window and the lady had the expression of "what idiot have we got today" written all over her face. Got it. I slotted the lens into the frame, put the glasses on and we were away.

The interview itself went well, and was over almost before it had started. I told a few stories relative to the book, and all was well. I had learned what an anecdote was! And in a way it was the start of my talks; a collection of anecdotes!

Another word which had the same effect on me when asked unexpectedly was 'troglodyte'. The question from the floor was simply, are there still troglodytes living on the Isle of Wight?

This was in year 2000! For a split second I froze, what the hell is a troglodyte? I had heard the word many times, but what did it mean? I started to answer the question, hoping the meaning would come, and sure enough, it did. I said, "I do not think so…" and then it came to me, a troglodyte is a cave dweller: "The last one was a man called 'Holy Joe' who lived in a cave at Ventnor, but he was evicted by the authorities many years ago." The questioner was highly impressed with my response; I quickly asked for another question!

It pays to have one's mind ready for any question, even before the talk begins. As is mentioned elsewhere, any fee I receive for a talk has always been donated to a local charity; it's my way of raising funds for these deserving causes. I have been asked to talk to a wide variety of organisations over the last 20 years, but I forgot where I was once. I had been asked to talk to a group from the mainland who came over to the Island once a year, a group of retired Inland Revenue (as it was then) Officers! I had been invited to a lunch before the talk, and in the general greetings which take place before such an event, I was asked if I did a lot of these talks. I replied honestly – "Yes, I get asked to do quite a lot, all over the Island." I was asked what my fee was, and I told him. "Do you declare it?" Remember, I was talking to a senior retired Inland Revenue Officer, and I had quite forgot! Luckily my mind clicked in. "I have a lot of expenses" says I. "Yes, I expect you do" was the disbelieving reply, given with a wink! The talk went well, but I have never forgotten to remember who my audience is since that time.

One of the traditions of the game is, firstly, the introduction before the talk starts and, secondly, the vote of thanks at the end. Sometimes these can be both lengthy, and boring; at other times they can be short and entertaining, but it does help if you have an introduction. I recall that on one occasion there was no introduction. I was just left standing at the front and had to start by introducing myself, and my talk, etc. At the time I had talks several times a week. I have my basic notes in a file ready for the next time; I check my diary for the venue and talk, and proceed to the event.

I gave my talk, one which I had done many times before, and felt it was strange that some people were not particularly interested. As I finished, after about 40 minutes, a voice from the audience was heard to say "we had that one last time!" I had looked at the wrong week in my diary. Now I always check first before giving a talk.

The vote of thanks is more interesting. I sometimes look around my audience to see if I can spot who has been selected to stand up and speak at the end of my talk. It is not difficult to identify that person; it is the one with a worried look on her/his face, and who may be jotting down a few notes. The problem is that usually the person who is taking notes will go on and on when it comes to the thanks! Sometimes I get it right. I remember one meeting where a lady was taking notes all through my talk (or so I thought). My thoughts were correct. As I finished, a voice was heard to say "Mrs. …..., will you give a vote of thanks to our speaker", and sure enough, that same person stood up, and gave the best vote of thanks I have ever had. She said "Thank you", and sat down. Now that is good advice to anyone who gets the task thrust upon them.

Over the years I have learned who gets the job at some venues, and one in particular is skilled at the task. Her thanks were always far better than any talk I gave, and nearly as long, so I used to leave ten minutes at the end for her words which were full of 'anecdotes'. She became a good friend over the years, and I am sure Doris Osborne from East Cowes will not mind me giving her name here. She always had wonderful stories.

I have given some television interviews over the years and I recall being stopped in Newport one day by a stranger who said she had seen me on the box the night before - "…talking to your relatives in Chale Churchyard!" She was referring to a recording I did in the churchyard, but my relatives were not very communicative!

I was once told that my new talk was "very good", the trouble was, at the time I had not given it to anyone. Now that is fame.

I spent many years running a charity fundraising stall which we took to many events around the Island every year. At one place, an elderly priest and his wife approached, and he offered to buy his wife a tombola ticket. She insisted she did not want one. He took no notice of his even older wife, who kept saying "No, No, I don't want one. No." Her husband bought a ticket, gave it to his wife, and she won. She was furious. The following year the same thing happened again, and she again insisted "No, I don't want one". He bought the ticket, and again she won. I never saw them again.

Many years ago there were what appeared to be two elderly spinster sisters who came to our stall. They had clearly just come from a Sunday church service, and were discussing the sermon. One said to the other "It's all wrong. The story about the missionary in Africa was very interesting, but you cannot have a 'black' missionary. Missionaries are 'white'. Whatever is the world coming to?"

I was in a supermarket car park one day when an elderly couple got out of a car with a young grandchild, aged about 4 years. The wife did not close the door correctly, and the little boy said "You silly old cow". She retorted "Wherever did you get that word from?" "It's what granddad calls you" he replied. Say no more, but just be careful what you say in the presence of children!

I did not like school, but it had its uses. Even before I started at the age of 5 years, I used to travel in my father's carriers van and often arrived outside the school when the children were going in, in the morning. One day it was my turn. I was too big for the seat I was given and had to have a larger one; the table was too small also. So when the end of the day came, I decided that that was enough and I would not go the next day. I soon realised there was more to come.

I was never very good at reading and still remember having to read one 'early' book out loud and could not say one particular word. Every time I had to go right back to the start of the book and begin again. I think it took all term before I got to the end.

School meals were also a problem. I was what was described as 'fussy', but it was tapioca which proved the greatest challenge and on more than one occasion I was not allowed to go out into the playground until I had finished this more objectionable of meals, and missed the whole break. In fact, with the food being cooked on the premises we did quite well, but I did not see it.

The arrival of the school dentist was another never to be forgotten event. He hurt, and I did not appreciate it. Any chance I could avoid school on dentist days was planned. I often feigned some illness to avoid school that day. That fear of a dentist still rules my life!

Being an only child of older parents, my early life was somewhat different from most children. I am not sure if it was by choice or requirement, but play was usually associated with work, and I did not mix much with those of a similar age. Toys were mainly tools; proper tools which a man used. I recall my mother telling me that for one Christmas an aunt gave me a wooden 'chopper' as part of a 'Red Indian' game – Cowboys and Indians was usual at the time, now somewhat frowned on! On opening the parcel I reacted by throwing it away; I was used to using a proper chopper to cut up wood, etc.! What good would that be? After that my Christmas and birthday presents were usually practical rather than for play.

Indeed, from as early as six my most enjoyable time was spent on a Sunday morning visiting the lady who lived in the house next door. She taught secretarial work, and she had a typewriter. A proper big one, with a bell and handles with which you could push the 'big roll' at the top from side to side, and keys which rattled. On Sunday mornings I was invited in to 'have a go on her typewriter'. She provided sheets of old paper and I would take home the results of my efforts to show Mum and Dad. From an early age I was destined to work in an office! And I wanted one of my own. They were far too expensive so I was told that if I wanted one I would have to save up for it. From that time every present I received was in the form of money. 6d or 1/-, and if I was very lucky, even a 2/6 (half crown) postal order. I never spent them, just saved the money to buy a typewriter!

I think I had accumulated just over £6, a substantial mount for a boy in the early 1950s, when my father said he had spoken to a lady who was selling a typewriter, did I want it? "Yes, Yes". My dreams were fulfilled. The problem was that it would cost £10, and I only had £6. If I promised to continue to save, he would buy it for me now. I had my typewriter! Before long I was typing my father's invoices! A year or two later, my status came to the notice of my school teacher. Our village school did not have a typewriter, and I was asked to type out small notices for school events such as a Jumble Sale or Concert using carbon paper so that I did six copies at one go! (What has happened to carbon paper? I do still have a box; no doubt it will be a 'Flog It' special one day!) This alone raised my status in the school, and I never looked back.

I mainly wish to forget school; I did not like it and it did not like me! And I must have been a horrible little creature. I was made 'bus prefect'; I collected the fare, usually 1d and bought all the tickets. At the next day's Assembly I had to stand up and tell of everyone who had been naughty. "… stood up, … shouted, … said a rude word". They hated me, and my chance of making new friends was quickly eliminated.

I will not dwell too long on school, as it pains me too much, but even when I tried to be helpful, it would go wrong. We had a School Fête, things to buy and sell, one of which was a guinea-pig, in its own box. It did not sell, and because my mother had not been able to go to the Sale, she gave my five shillings, Yes, 5/-, to buy things left over the next day, and if I wanted it I could spend 2/6d on the guinea-pig and box. I have always been a careful creature, but could not find anything worth buying, except the guinea-pig. I spent the whole sum on guinea-pig and box. I even took it home on the bus.

When I got home all was well until I said it had cost me the whole 5/-, then I was in trouble. Big trouble. In those days we had a travelling grocer who came to our house once a week, and he used an old ambulance as his vehicle. He was Mr. Guy. I liked Mr. Guy; he always had a smile and patted me on the head. Mr. Guy was there this day. My mother said to him "Look what Derek has done; and how much do you think he has paid for it?" Mr. Guy thought for a moment or two, and then said "Well, it must be worth £1.1/- (a Guinea)". I was off the hook! Mr. Guy was my friend for life!

In those days, one could buy an Oxo Cube (to make gravy, etc.) for 1d each. Mr. Guy's bill always came to something and 11d, i.e. 5/11d, or 6/11d. He always added one Oxo to the bill and made the cost up to a round shilling! We had dozens of Oxo Cubes in the cupboard, and even when my Mother passed on, there was still a box of Oxos in her cupboard!

Not wishing to dwell any longer on school, I will conclude with my memories when King George VI died. We were at school when the news came through. For some months, a special visit to see a film in a cinema, in Ryde, had been planned, and the opportunity for a day's afternoon off school, and a coach trip to boot, had been awaited with enthusiasm. Then we heard, because the King had died, the trip was off'! "Bu..er, the King… etc. He's gone and spoilt our day!" Then we heard the trip might be arranged later, so not so bad after all.

Then the practicalities of the event came across our minds. Had the world come to an end? What was going to happen to us? Every morning at Assembly we sang "God Save the King". Now we would have to sing "God Save the Queen", and that seemed wrong. Our simple lives were in turmoil. Everyone was looking sad and mournful; I think they stopped the busses, so we went home early (not so bad now, good old King, pity he didn't die more often!).

Over the following weeks we had the funeral. I kept a scrap book of every picture in the newspapers, and I still have it to this day. No television then; just the radio.

And then we heard the film was to be shown again, and our trip was on again. The anticipated day arrived and we all set off in a bus, to Ryde. Well, if I say that the film was an opera called 'The Tales of Hoffman' by Offenbach, especially made for Junior School children to educate them into the world of classical opera, you will realise we were not happy! It was the most boring afternoon any of us had ever had! God Save the King.

Oh Yes, before we leave Junior School for ever, just a peculiar thing about my school. Whenever there was a School Concert, or Special Day, a large audience of parents and grandparents would gather for the occasion, but what was different was that it was mainly made up of fathers and grandfathers, not so many mothers. You see, our teacher was quite a buxom lady. You know, she carried all before her. She also loved playing the piano, which was always placed sideways on to the audience. This way she could see everyone, and they could see most of her. She played by raising her hands and arms high into the air before each note which would be thumped with some enthusiasm.

The fact that she usually wore a low-cut dress (for the occasion) had the effect that probably more was visible than normal, and certainly more than the war weary men of Chale had experienced for some time, if ever. And she knew it. The farther they leaned forward to observe the bouncing orbs, the more she leaned forward, and the more energetically she played. Did I hear 'Encore'? Well, the music part usually went on for quite a while!

On Friday afternoons, the older boys were required to 'read' to our teacher, at her desk. In turn we would be called out to view the pages; her arm reaching round our waists pulling these young innocent boys ever closer to her, as ever, revealing chest until we had a clear view. It was amazing how much we looked forward to Friday afternoons in those days, but no doubt it added to our education. Those were the days!

When I left Chale School, every school leaver received a copy of the book 'Back of the Wight' by Fred Mew, B.E.M., C.C., who was the Chairman of the School Managers as well as a local historian, author, and former Gold Professional at Chale Golf Club. I still have my copy, signed by him, and also by our Head Teacher. It is inscribed 'To Derek Sprake, for fine work in the school, generally, and for valued assistance." July 1953. As someone once remarked, "She could not think of anything specific that you were good at!"

Looking back I am actually lucky to be here at all. When my parents married they did not live together at first. It was the early part of WW2 and the invasion could have happened at any time. So my mother continued to live in the house where she had lived with her parents in Newport, and my father lived in his home at Chale. He used to visit her on Saturday evenings, and 'stay over' until Sunday morning. This went on for some 6 months, until my grandfather died, then my mother moved to Chale. This was not a satisfactory arrangement. She had always lived in a town, and was never happy living in the country. After some months, she packed her bags and went back to Newport to stay with her sister; but was told to "get on with life; you are married to him and you must put up with it".

My mother returned home and I was born nine months later!

Something must have happened? I sometimes include this story in a talk, and on one occasion there was an elderly lady in the audience who had known my mother quite well. At the end she came over to me and asked if my mother had had Cream Crackers that night? Enquiring what she meant, she said my mother had admitted to her that she always had two Cream Crackers after having sex (presumably with my father). Now this was a surprise to me; it was not a subject which my parents talked about. But then I thought ……..

Because he was a Carrier, my father always did the shopping and brought home the items required. On a Friday I did recall that he always brought home two packets of Cream Cracker biscuits, irrespective of how many there were left in the larder. Indeed, when she eventually died, there were still a number of old packets of Cream Crackers in her kitchen; my father had died 30 years before! Clearly this was her 'turn-on' which was their secret signal! I was asked by one person to whom I told this (true) story, what did she do with the crumbs? I leave that to the readers' imagination.

In giving the talks, I am usually sent a letter or agenda giving the order of events, and indicating where my talk would fit in. A comment on one referred to the fact that "we do our business first!" The English language has many words with differing meanings, and the word 'business' is one of those. Someone 'in business' can be said to be self-employed, the expression, 'mind your business' usually means 'keep your nose out', and 'doing your business' can mean a visit to the toilet. It was reassuring that these ladies would be doing their business before I was asked to speak!

There was a time when you had to write a letter or a Post Card to send a message; then the telephone changed all that; by the second half of the 20th century the use of an answerphone meant that you could leave a message when the person was not there. This has now been replaced again, by fax machines, and now the internet. To many people, the fact that you might be having your message recorded, and there was no immediate reply or acknowledgement on the 'phone, was a daunting experience. I had one message from an elderly lady, for whom the answerphone was all too much.

After a short period of silence her voice came over, starting with a hesitant "Oh, dear", then again and again "Oh, dear; Oh, dear". I recognised the voice but I could not help. Eventually she started to leave a message, again interspersed with the repeated "Oh, dear". Later I 'phoned the caller and she admitted she hated talking on those horrible things!

Standing in a shop where the telephone continually rang, and no-one answered it, one person waiting to be served and clearly annoyed by the ringing shouted in a loud voice "If you pick up the bl…y receiver and say hello, it will stop ringing". And it did!

I once went to Canada for a short holiday. On the flight back, I got into conversation with the gentleman sitting next to me. The Isle of Wight came up; yes he had been there once – to the big Pop Festival at Freshwater (we chatted about that), etc. Eventually I asked him where he had been, and why he had gone to Canada. "Oh, it's been a complete waste of time." Curious, I enquired why? "I have been to visit my father-in-law" he said. "We had had an urgent call to say he was dying so I rushed over for the funeral. I took my funeral suit and all … After a couple of days he suddenly got better. A complete waste of time!" Some people are never satisfied.

One of the bonuses of giving a talk, particularly to such as a Women's Institute, is that the speaker is provided with some refreshment; usually a cup-of-tea, some sandwiches, and a piece of cake. I have learned that if you do not eat too quickly there is often a bit of cake left over, and hating waste, I, well, am happy to dispose of it. But sometimes even the best planned meeting can go wrong. At one such event, a full tea was laid out with plates, knives, cups, saucers, spoons, etc. The sugar for the beverage was as usual in a nice cut-glass bowl with spoon. I took what I needed and stirred the drink vigorously. The first sip indicated there was something wrong; it was salt. I mentioned the fact to the host, who assured me it was not her, but someone else who had put the salt in the sugar bowl! It was soon replaced, but whenever I partook of a cup-of-tea again, I always sampled the sugar first!

One teacher, trying to educate her pupils to speak 'proper English' insisted her young students used the proper name for an animal. A cat was a 'cat', not a 'pussy'; a dog was not a 'bow-wow', a sheep was not a 'baa-baa', etc. One attentive boy, who was seen to be reading a new book by A.A. Milne, was asked "What are you reading?" "Winnie-the-Shite" he replied.

And talking of cows, I remember whilst serving on a fundraising stall where there were various stuffed toy animals as prizes and the winner could choose the item he wanted, he said he wanted "the little cow". Asked why, he said it reminded him of his Mum. I enquired why was that? "Well, it's what my Dad calls her." And on another occasion at a fête, a little girl came along dressed as a Princess for the fancy dress parade. Enquiring, "… are you a Princess?" her brother replied for her "No, that's my sister!"

I am always amused when a planned event goes slightly wrong. I remember some years ago when I was in Guernsey for their Liberation day celebrations, to mark the end of the German occupation on 9th May 1945. The Queen was attending and there was a large crowd gathering at a local sports centre. I always aim to get to an event such as this early to get a good vantage point; the best is often near where the T.V. cameras are positioned.

I arrived before most, and preparation work was about to start. Firstly they checked the flag mast which was to be used to raise the Royal Standard when the Queen arrived. The wheel at the top was stuck, and the only way was to remove the whole pole and fix another. Then it was noticed someone had left a bicycle chained to a post just outside the main door exactly where the Queen was to enter the Centre. The owner could not be found and in the end a policeman had to cut the chain with metal cutters and the bike was taken away to cheers. Then a policeman noticed I had a bag (which contained my lunch etc.) and it was searched to ensure there was no bomb!

Eventually the invited guests started to arrive; then groups of representatives from local organisations; and a small military band. As usual there were half a dozen members of the Chelsea Pensioners resplendent in their red uniforms. The band played some military tunes, and all was ready.

At the anticipated hour, a motorbike outrider was seen at the end of the approach road, followed by a posh car with tinted windows and a small flag fixed to the bonnet. The assembled groups were called to attention; the Royal Standard was raised; the band was prepared, and the Bandmaster raised his arms with baton erect. Union flags were energetically waved.

The car slowly advanced, and stopped just at the start of the parade, and the door opened. The band were prepared; the baton raised. The National Anthem commenced as a smart female leg came from the car. Everyone cheered. A very smart lady of mature age got out and then people started to speak; "that does not look like Her Majesty?" No, it was not her! "So who is it?" One local person said, "That's the Bailiffs wife!" Then everyone started to laugh, as did the lady. The band master, a rather short portly soldier, continued to play the National Anthem and then quickly gave orders in a loud voice "Stop playing" "At ease".

The whole event was now turning into a comedy. However, about five minutes later there appeared another outrider, another 'posh' car with a royal flag on the bonnet. Was this the one?

This time the band waited until they were certain the Queen had indeed arrived, and as she stepped out of her car there was a loud cry "Band, attention! And for the second time, lets play the National Anthem". The band struck up, and everyone laughed. I wonder if the Queen wondered why there was such hilarity for her arrival. Then Prince Philip also alighted from the limousine. The Royal guests walked slowly along the paraded ranks and spoke to some, but soon the Queen was walking quite alone over to the front door of the Centre, when it appeared she realised that Prince Philip was not there. She looked round to see he was chatting to the Chelsea Pensioners! And he continued to chat to them for quite a long time whilst his wife was left standing waiting for him. Calls of "she's waiting for you" and similar had no effect. Eventually he got to her side, waving to the crowd, and they went inside.

It was then announced that the public could meet the Queen when she came out from the Service, at the rear entrance where metal barriers were erected, but where no-one was waiting. Perhaps a notice "No admittance" to this area was to blame. So we went round and stood in the front row. The Queen, Prince Philip and other dignitaries came out and she started talking to us mortals. She was coming towards me; would she speak to me? My hand started to shake. What should I say to her? And yes, she stopped right in front of me, and spoke to me! "Isn't it a lovely day!" She said – It was a beautiful day. My mouth opened to greet her, but for the first time in my life, nothing came out. All I could do was stand, mouth open, and I nodded in agreement. She smiled (or was she laughing) at me, and she moved on. My one and only chance to speak to our gracious Queen had gone – for ever. But I have never forgotten that wonderful day.

To finish this chapter, I thought the reader might be amused by the Parable of the 'isms' (the two cows).

SOCIALISM - If you have two cows you give one to your neighbour.

COMMUNISM - If you have two cows you give them to the government and the government gives you some milk.

FASCISM – If you have two cows you keep the cows and give the milk to the government. Then the government sells you some milk.

NEW DEALISM (USA in the 1930s) – If you have two cows you shoot one and milk the other. Then you pour the milk down the drain.

NAZISM – If you have two cows the government shoots you and keeps the cows.

CAPITALISM – If you have two cows you sell one and buy a bull !!!

CHAPTER 12
The Audience

I trust that this summary of some of the talks I have given over the years has proved of interest, just as I hope my talks have given pleasure to my audiences, which have varied greatly! If they have made you smile now and again, then I am happy! The success of any talk depends so much on the audience and their response, and I can honestly say that my audiences over the last twenty years have given me much pleasure (usually!) and without them it would not have been possible. Speakers, as we are often called, provide a unique type of entertainment coupled with factual information and historical accounts of events on our Island. I wish to end this book by paying tribute to my audiences.

I have found that an all female audience of perhaps elderly ladies enjoy them as much as any, and it needs a different style of talk for a male audience! Their sense of humour is somehow different. Most groups are of people born and bred on the Isle of Wight so that one does not have to explain where places are, but I must say that more and more contain Overners (people from the mainland who have come over the sea to live on our Island). One might expect them to be less knowledgeable about our Island, but that was a trap I first fell into when I was asked to talk about our Island to visitors with SAGA Holidays, some years ago.

Clearly the age of my audience was going to be over 60, and later, over 50, so I prepared a talk aimed at that age group. I had been told that someone from SAGA would 'drop in' from time to time to ensure my talk was up to their required standards. In fact the 'judge' was known to me when she arrived although not introduced as such. Well, so I thought. The second talk started when a 'young lady' (20s) arrived wearing a short mini-skirt and whereas most of the audience had sat some way back, she sat in the front row. She crossed her legs in a provocative way and I have to admit for the first time ever, I was slightly thrown.

My mind passed from my prepared script and I was unsure of myself. Even more so in that she looked straight into my eyes. Was she the 'someone' sent to judge me? My worst fears engulfed me and I was hesitating. Was this a lady from SAGA? I recovered my senses and got back on cue – and then this vision of beauty and confusion got up and walked out! To this day I do not know who she was or indeed why she had been sent to tempt me. I have to admit that I think she had gone to the wrong room and was probably as confused as I was. However, what it did was to teach me to be prepared for anything; but I did enjoy it while it lasted!

My talks to SAGA Holidays lasted several years; mainly one a week in the early months and the later months of the holiday season. What it did do was to make me prepared for anything, and over the years I am no longer affected by what appears before me!

What I have discovered is that whilst most people sit in rows towards the back, and rarely in the front row, those who do fill the front seats have no fears as to what they show. The speaker is in a vulnerable position to have the best view of what is on offer, and this can vary according to the person's age. Why do some people spread their legs whilst occupying the front row, and reveal perhaps more than is totally necessary? Rather like the young lady at my SAGA meeting, it does detract from what one is supposed to be doing, and it can basically 'put one off'!

On arriving at the hotel where these talks were given one evening, I was met by two eccentric old ladies who asked if I knew when the talk started. They added that they had been told it was 'very good'; they did not know it was me! I said that I had heard the same. They were looking forward to the evening. By the time designated to start, and with the audience waiting, the two ladies had not arrived. I eventually went in search of them and found that they had had a drink, and gone to sleep!

Going to sleep is fairly normal and it is rare when giving a talk that at least one person has not nodded off. However, there was one occasion when everyone went to sleep! It was held in the lounge of the hotel, where the chairs were particularly comfortable. The outside temperature was warm, and the central heating had been switched on. It was held just after lunch, and I had nearly nodded off when I sat down to await my audience. Within five minutes of starting my talk, everyone was fast asleep. It is not just the closing of the eyes; it is the general relaxation of the whole body! The legs come open, the arms flop, and the head goes back, with the effect that the mouth comes open, and the occasional snore can be detected.

What does one do in these circumstances. Stop talking? Or just continue as if nothing had happened? Or talk a little louder and hope that someone will wake up? I tried the latter and some did respond, even if temporarily. I reached the end which was greeted with applause, and everyone said they had enjoyed the talk, which proves you do not need to be awake to hear voices!

My first experience of 'slumber' was early on, when an elderly and somewhat frail lady was helped into the room by a friend. I was asked if she could sit near me so she could hear as she was looking forward to the talk (I think it was 'Put Out The Flag' – she remembered the Carrier coming to her house years ago). She was positioned in a chair beside me. As I commenced the talk I noticed that her head nodded forward and her chin rested on her chest; her mouth came open, etc. She was out! Assuring myself that she was still alive, I completed the talk, some 40 minutes or so. Warm applause greeted the final words which clearly brought our dear friend back to the living, she smiled and said how much she enjoyed it!

I have learned that talks in the afternoon, particularly following lunch, are the worst for the audience falling asleep, so I now try to avoid such times. After dinner talks, in the evening do not seem so vulnerable, and tend to be shorter. The greatest problem here is if alcohol has been consumed in the interval; I think it was in such circumstances that the only time I stopped my talk and actually walked out. I was getting silly unacceptable comments from an adult audience, both insulting to their fellow members, and to me! I said, "Sorry, you don't want to listen to me, and I don't want to listen to you". I walked out and refused my fee, despite a very embarrassed Chairman protesting and making profuse apologies!

Humour can come in various forms, and it depends on the audience how far one can go. It is not necessary to be rude to make people laugh, but sometimes a slight mild swear is acceptable! Even to a female audience. But there is always the risk you will upset someone, it is par for the course. I recall a meeting in Yarmouth with a full room of mature women. I included some of my usual stories. Most seemed to enjoy it, but two ladies, sitting in the front row, were clearly not amused! On the way out, after the talk, I found myself walking behind these two ladies, who were deep in conversation about something. One looked round at me, and said to her friend, "Look out, he's behind us". They hurried on ahead and disappeared!

I was not invited back to that group for some five years, and I assumed that I had indeed upset someone. Then, out of the blue I got a call to come again and give another talk. With some trepidation I went along, and after such a time presumed that my elderly dissenters had probably passed on, or at least had advanced in age and would not be there. I moved to the lectern provided for me and scanned the audience; were they there? Yes they were, in the front row just in front of me, and looking me in the eye! But this time, they appeared to enjoy every part of my talk and led the laughter. Time has a way of mellowing some people. They even clapped hands at the end.

Sleep is one thing, death is another, and on at least one occasion I became aware that one lady in the audience appeared to have died. Well, she suddenly slumped forward onto the table in front of her. Her face turned a dull grey colour and she still was not moving. That looked a bit fatal to me. The others on her table did not seem to be worried, but I asked "Is she OK?". "Oh yes, it's just the blood!" I could not remember any reference to blood in my talk, and as I was nearly at the end, I asked if I should stop. "No, no" was the reply, "it's too interesting!". I continued, and slowly the colour returned to the lady's face, she raised her head, and sat back in her chair. Later I enquired after her health, to be told she had given blood that afternoon and it always affected her that way, but she did not want to miss my talk.

I have had the pleasure of talking at most of the numerous small halls around the Isle of Wight and they vary in size and shape. Some are long and narrow, and the rear of the audience may be some distance from the front. More and more now use microphones and the loop system for the hard-of-hearing, but one often has to use one's voice to ensure everyone can hear. I recall at one narrow venue, I almost had to shout to ensure those at the back could hear; I was told I was too loud for those in the

172 AN ISLE OF WIGHT RACONTEUR

front! In fact I am often thanked because 'we can hear you'; not always the case with some speakers.

I have only once spoken on the mainland. I was invited to a village in Sussex. A delightful group. It was the talk on smuggling, so I took along maps and other details of the Isle of Wight so I could clearly indicate the places to which I was referring. At the end, an old lady said, "I thought they did smuggling at Rye in East Sussex". I explained that they did, but I was talking about smuggling on the Isle of Wight. "Oh", she said, "did they do smuggling there too!" I was not asked back!

The most enjoyable meetings are when everyone joins in; there is a little banter; and I am flooded with questions. It's even better when applause and cheers ring out, and it does happen sometimes.

Sometimes I make slightly derogative comments about the French (well, they were traditionally our enemies throughout much of the eighteenth and nineteenth centuries). It was not until one day that a lady in a blue and white hooped jumper suddenly leapt up when I made my usual comment about the French, and in a strong French accent, proclaimed "I am French". Luckily she had a broad grin on her face, and at the end she said she had enjoyed our banter. "I hope you come again!".

Returning to the SAGA talks, I had assumed that as all my audience was from the mainland, some even from abroad, they would have little knowledge of the Isle of Wight. How wrong I was; indeed they had read all the books and often knew more than I did about us. One gentleman said he used to visit the Island before the First World War (he must have been very young) and that his family always stayed at a farm where they hired bicycles. "Is the farm still there?" he asked. I asked where it was, but he could not remember; which part of the Island did they stay, he could not remember? I concluded the discussion by saying "Yes, I remember where you stayed. Sadly it has closed down now but it was near Bembridge". He said "Yes, that's it; thank you" and he went off happily to bed.

One lady insisted I start my talk at the advertised time (8.30 p.m.) even though people were still coming into the room. She would not wait for them. I found out later that she had tried to make the coach driver drive off before all the passengers had got on during a coach trip that afternoon. Another person challenged every item I told them. I eventually made a totally untrue statement and asked him if that was right. He replied that he did not know. The whole audience gave a cheer, and he never interrupted me again. I learned afterwards that he did the same to coach drivers on outings, but after that he was no problem!

Some organisations ask the speakers to do other tasks whilst there, such as judging a small competition. They try to choose a subject close to the theme of the talk. Even so, there is also a 'Best Bloom' to judge. Here my previous horticultural knowledge comes in useful. Sometimes it is even to judge a cake! Well, I love cakes. I recall once, it was to judge a scone. There were four there, most looked really good, but one was rather flat and slightly burned. The trouble was that that one tasted absolutely wonderful; the rest not so good! Much to the obvious annoyance of several 'experts' there I chose the poor looking one. It tasted the best. I was never asked to judge scones again!

But in the end it is the pure enjoyment I get from my role as a speaker on the Isle of Wight. I hope this book will encourage others to come along to future talks. See you there.

CASHIER 1

It's bloody cold down here Mildred!